MARK DEVER

# CHURCH ESSENTIALS

WHAT IS A HEALTHY CHURCH?

Curriculum developed by Bobby Jamieson

LifeWay Press®
Nashville, Tennessee

Published by LifeWay Press®


ISBN 978-1-4158-7182-9
Item 005467768

Dewey decimal classification: 250
Subject heading: CHURCH



To order additional copies of this resource, write to LifeWay Church Resources Customer Service; One LifeWay Plaza; Nashville, TN 37234-0113; fax (615) 251-5933; phone toll free (800) 458-2772; e-mail *orderentry@lifeway.com;* order online at *www.lifeway.com;* or visit the LifeWay Christian Store serving you.

*Printed in the United States of America*

Leadership and Adult Publishing
LifeWay Church Resources
One LifeWay Plaza
Nashville, TN 37234-0175

# Contents

# About the Author

**Mark Dever** serves as the senior pastor of Capitol Hill Baptist Church in Washington, DC. Since first serving as a pastor in 1985, Mark has served on the pastoral staffs of four churches, including a church plant in Massachusetts. Prior to moving to Washington in 1994, Mark taught for the faculty of Divinity at Cambridge University while serving for two years as an associate pastor of Eden Baptist Church.

Currently, Mark serves as the president of 9Marks in Washington, D.C. He also teaches periodically at various conferences, speaking everywhere from South Africa to Brazil to the United Kingdom to Alabama. Feeling a deep burden for pastors, Mark often addresses pastors conferences and teaches at seminaries.

He has served as a trustee of The Southern Baptist Theological Seminary, a member of the council of the Alliance of Confessing Evangelicals, and a board member of The Gospel Coalition. From 1995 until 2001, he served on the steering committee for Founders Ministries. As Guest Senate Chaplain for two weeks in 1995, Mark opened the daily sessions of the United States Senate in prayer. He is a member of the American Society of Church History and the Tyndale Fellowship, and he held the J.B. Lightfoot Scholarship at Cambridge University from 1989 to 1991.

Mark has authored multiple books, including

- *Richard Sibbes: Puritanism and Calvinism in Late Elizabethan and Early Stuart England* (2000)
- *Nine Marks of a Healthy Church* (orig. 2001; 4 editions; 9 translations)
- *Polity: Biblical Arguments on How to Conduct Church Life* (2001), editor
- *The Deliberate Church: Building Your Ministry on the Gospel* (2005), coauthored with Paul Alexander
- *Message of the New Testament: Promises Kept* (2006)
- *Message of the Old Testament: Promises Made* (2007)
- *What is a Healthy Church?* (2007)
- *The Gospel and Personal Evangelism* (2008)
- *In My Place Condemned He Stood* (2008), coauthored with J.I. Packer
- *Twelve Challenges Churches Face* (2009)
- *What Does God Want of Us Anyway?* (2010)
- *It Is Well* (2010), coauthored with Michael Lawrence

Additionally, Mark has a been contributing editor to the Cambridge Papers, and his works have been published in the Journal of Ecclesiastical History, Christian Arena magazine, the Founders Journal, Leadership Journal, Regeneration Quarterly, Modern Reformation, The Southern Baptist Journal of Theology, Tabletalk, the Disciple's Study Bible, and Building on a Sure Foundation. He has also contributed an article on John L. Dagg to Theologians of the Baptist Tradition. More recently, he has contributed to many books including *The Compromised Church*, *Give Praise to God: A Vision for Reforming Worship*, *Christ and His Church*, and *Sex and the Supremacy of Christ*. He also has articles in *Reforming Pastoral Ministry, Why I am a Baptist*, and *The Westminster Confession into the 21st Century, vol. 1*.

Mark received his Doctor of Philosophy in Ecclesiastical History from Cambridge University. He also holds a Master of Theology from The Southern Baptist Theological Seminary, a Master of Divinity, summa cum laude, from Gordon-Conwell Theological Seminary, and a Bachelor of Arts, magna cum laude, from Duke University.

He and his wife Connie live and minister on Capitol Hill in Washington, D.C. They have two adult children.

**Bobby Jamieson** serves 9Marks as assistant editor and website manager. After graduating from the University of Southern California, Jamieson was a pastoral intern at Capitol Hill Baptist Church in Washington, DC. He is currently a MDiv student at Southern Seminary, and he lives with his wife and daughter in Louisville, Kentucky.

## What are you looking for in a church?

You might not have thought about that question lately. But take a moment now to ask yourself, *What does the ideal church look like?*

Is the music the most important aspect to you? Is the deciding factor in choosing a church what types of instruments they play or the kinds of songs they sing? Worship is obviously an important part of what happens in a church.

But maybe music isn't as important to you as the preaching. You want a church where the sermons are good: meaningful, but not heavy-handed; biblical, but not boring; practical, but not picky and legalistic. No doubt the preaching is important, too.

Or perhaps you're looking for a church where you can easily relate to the people because they're in the same stage of life as you. You want other young families, retirees, or unmarried people so you have a built in point of connection. God wants us to live in community with each other, right?

Maybe the ministries of the church are important to you. You want a place that has a vibrant children's ministry, a consistent outreach to the community, a chance to be involved in helping the poor, or lots of activities for youth. Surely these are good opportunities for a church to provide.

Or maybe you're just looking for a church that feels a certain way. You can't put your finger on it, but you know it when you're there. It's an environment where you feel both challenged and encouraged, convicted and uplifted. It's a home for you and others.

These are all fine attributes, but are they essential? Are they the most vital parts of church life that add up to a healthy church? That's the question of this study. In the following pages, you'll find the answer to the question of what makes a healthy church.

Note, however, that the question is about *health*. It's not about preference, enjoyment, style, or trend. These are the marks that make a church healthy from a biblical standpoint, the attributes ingrained in every part of church life. It is our prayer that this study will be very useful in helping you be an active part of such a church—one that models and reflects the character and desire of God.

# Here's How the Study Works:

This study includes opportunities for both individual and group study. Engaging in the individual daily devotions and then participating in a Bible study group, which includes video teaching and discussion, is the best way to gain the fullest understanding of *Church Essentials.*

At the beginning of each session, you will find the guide for the Bible study group portion of the study. Each meeting should follow this general outline:

**Getting Started:** Begin each week with a set of questions designed to help you and your group get to know each other better and process what the Lord has been teaching you over the previous week (20 min.).

**View DVD Segment:** Your group will watch a video segment from the DVD while filling in the listening guide provided in this book (30 min.).

**Group Response:** After the video segment, your group will discuss the truths you've seen presented in the group experience. Then you will close with prayer.

The video segment and group response will propel you forward, as an individual, into your study throughout the week. Each day, you'll continue looking at the Scriptures and ideas presented in your group by completing the five personal devotions. The next week, you will come back to your group ready to begin another discussion based on the individual work you've done.

Throughout these six sessions, you'll begin to catch a vision for what the church is meant to be. By God's grace, you'll fall in love all over again with the wonders of what God is building in His people, and be empowered to be a member of a healthy church.

1

# A Vision for Healthy Churches:

## *Expositional Preaching*

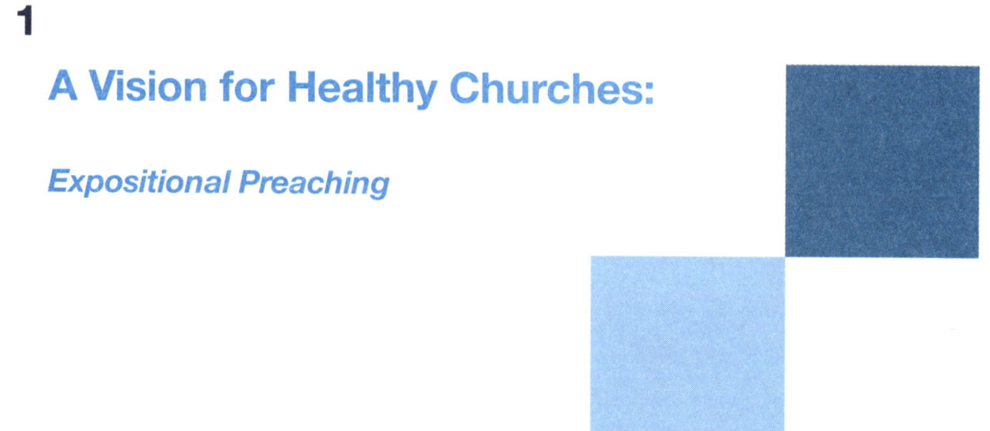

## Getting Started

**Welcome to the first small-group discussion of *Church Essentials.***

1 Introduce yourself to the group by sharing:

- Your name and brief information about your family;
- Where you spend most of your time during the week (home, school, business, etc.);
- And why you chose to participate in this study.

2 What do you think makes a church healthy?

3 Share with the group one experience you've had at church that you would consider to be "healthy." How did it impact your life?

4 Imagine that you just moved to a new town and you're looking for a new church. What's at the top of your list of the most important things you look for in a church?

## View DVD Segment

**Watch the segment from the DVD using the viewer guide below.**

Both the service and the congregation are important in __________________ the significance of the church.

As Christians what we can be confident of is the __________ of the gospel.

God is showing the fullness of His character through the local ___________.

There has been a ______________ of church just to evangelism.

A personal relationship with Jesus Christ can never be ____________.

The most important aspect of a church is whether it _____________ the gospel.

A healthy church _____________ what God is like.

Expositional preaching is _______________ and _____________ God's Word to God's people.

God's Word has always _________ God's people.

A church that realizes that God has spoken will make preaching ____________.

Church members should come ___________.

**Video sessions are available for purchase at lifeway.com/9marks**

## Group Response

**Discuss the segment with your group using the questions below.**

1 Why do you come to church? How does that affect what you put into church—and get out of it?

2 Do you think that church should play an important role in your life as a Christian? Why or why not?

3 In the interview Mark Dever said that a healthy church is one that reflects the character of God, and the way a church becomes more healthy is by listening to and obeying God's Word. What do you think about that definition of a healthy church?

4 How has the preaching in your church impacted your life?

5 Think back to the question we discussed before watching the video: "What are the most important things you would look for in a church?" Has your answer to that question changed because of this discussion? If so, how?

6 What do you think is standing in the way of your church becoming more biblically healthy? What can you do to help overcome those obstacles?

**Close with prayer.**

## Session One

## A Vision for Healthy Churches

Many Christians today tend to view their Christianity as a personal relationship with God and not much else. They generally know that this "personal relationship" has some implications for how they should live. But those same Christians often don't realize how this most important relationship with God necessitates a number of secondary personal relationships—the relationships that Christ establishes between us and His body, the church.

Despite popular opinion, an ongoing and participatory relationship to the church is not optional for a Christian. Healthy churches teach this. Healthy church members understand and love it. To begin to have that understanding, though, we must begin to see what the church really is ... and is not.

# 1
# Church Matters

For some Christians, participating in church compares pretty closely with cleaning the bathroom. It's boring and mildly unpleasant. Sometimes it's even a little painful with all that bending and scrubbing. But it's one of those things you just have to do.

For other Christians, church is one among dozens of dishes in the "Christian Growth Buffet." Along with Bible study groups, retreats, and sermon podcasts, church is one of many other options for how they might seek to grow in their walks with the Lord. And like the cheese grits at the breakfast buffet, one might decide to partake one week and skip it the next depending on what else is available.

For the former group, church doesn't seem to do that much good. For the latter, it has its purposes, but it's not that big a deal if you drop in and out at will since there are plenty of other options to choose from.

Would you say that you fit into either of these groups? If not—and they're certainly not the only ones—how would you say that you approach church participation?

How important is the church for your life as a Christian?

What difference do you think it makes whether or not a Christian actively participates in church?

According to Scripture, church matters. Participating in it shouldn't feel like drudgery, and it shouldn't simply be a side dish we skip when we've already got a full plate. Rather, the church should be central in our lives for two reasons: because God has made it central in His plan of salvation and because He has made it the central location for our growth as Christians.

**Church: At the Center of God's Saving Plan**

From the beginning of creation, God has been about creating a people for Himself. He didn't just create Adam, but Adam and Eve, who would then bring forth more people (Gen. 1:27-28). When He called Abraham, He promised to multiply him into a great nation (Gen. 12:1-3). Hundreds of years later, He led the entire people of Israel out of Egypt and into the land he promised them, taking them for His treasured possession (Ex. 19:5-6).

When Jesus came, He didn't just speak to individuals, but called twelve to be His disciples (Mark. 3:14). And after He died, rose again, and ascended into heaven, Jesus sent His disciples into all the earth not only to preach the gospel to individuals, but to gather them into churches (see the whole book of Acts!).

Read Ephesians 3:10-11. According to this passage, what is God's purpose for the church?

Who is God's wisdom put on display for, according to this passage?

Do you tend to think of your Christianity as something just between you and God? In what specific ways does Paul's teaching in this passage challenge that?

If the church is so central to God's saving plan, how might your life reflect that priority as well?

The church should be at the center of our lives as Christians because it's at the center God's saving plan.

## Church: At the Center of Christian Growth

The church should also be at the center of our lives because it's central for Christian growth.

Read Ephesians 4:11-16. For what purpose has God given pastors and teachers (vv. 11-12)? How do Christians grow up into Christ (vv. 15-16)?

In this passage Paul teaches that the church is central to how we grow as Christians. God gave pastors and teachers to build up the body of Christ (vv. 11-12) so that all of us would help each other grow in faith and knowledge (v. 13) until we all grow up to maturity in Christ (vv. 13-16). The primary means by which we grow in Christ is the ministry of pastors, teachers, and all of our fellow believers in the local church.

What are some specific ways you have grown in godliness through your local church?

On a scale of 1 to 10, how involved would you say you are in your local church? How do you think this has impacted your growth as a Christian?

Think of one concrete step you can take to grow in Christ through your church and to help someone else in your church grow in Christ. Pray that God would enable you to take these steps this week.

Church matters because it is at the center of God's saving plan and the center of Christian growth. As a believer in Christ, what will you do this week to put the church closer to the center of your life?

# 2

# Image is Everything

Most of the time, telling sickness from health is pretty easy. If you've got a 102.7 degree fever, chills, and can't even sit up straight in bed, you know you're pretty sick.

On the other hand, if you bounce out of bed in the morning, run ten miles before breakfast, work at full speed all day, and then spend two hours in the gym in the evening, you're probably on the healthier end of the spectrum.

But what about the health and sickness of local churches? How can you tell a healthy church from a not-so-healthy one?

How would you identify a healthy church? What are some of the characteristics it would have?

What about a not-so-healthy church? What are some signs of sickness in a local church?

## Image Is Everything

When we turn to Scripture to see what makes a church healthy, we find that image is everything. Not image as in the church's physical appearance, or what people wear, but the imaging of *God*.

God created man in His image to represent His character and rule (Gen. 1:26-28). That's what it means to be created in God's image; humans were intended to reflect the glory of God into all creation. But our first parents rebelled against Him, and all of us have rebelled against God ever since. However, Christ came into the world as the true image of God (Col. 1:15). He imaged God perfectly by carrying out God's will, including bearing the penalty for our failure to image God as we ought. Now he calls us, as individual believers and local churches, to reflect His glorious character to the world.

In yesterday's study we considered Paul's statement that through the church, God's wisdom is made known even to heavenly beings (Eph. 3:10-11). How do we make God's wisdom known? By reflecting his character.

Consider 2 Corinthians 3:18:

> ***We all, with unveiled faces, are looking as in a mirror at the glory of the Lord and are being transformed into the same image from glory to glory; this is from the Lord who is the Spirit.***

To grow as an individual Christian is to grow in reflecting the glory of the character of the Lord. The same thing is true for churches.

### A Healthy Church Is ...

In light of all this, here's how we could define a healthy church: *A healthy church is a congregation that increasingly reflects God's character as His character has been revealed in His Word.*

Name several different aspects of God's character. How could those character traits be concretely displayed in your church?

What are some ways that others in your church have ministered to you recently? How did their actions reflect God's character?

List three common problems in churches. Is your church facing any of these right now? How would a focus on reflecting God's character impact these issues?

1

2

3

**... One that Increasingly Reflects God's Character ...**

Remember that a healthy church is one that *increasingly* reflects God's character. No church is perfectly holy, so no church perfectly reflects God's character. But a healthy church is one in which the individual members, and the church as a whole, are consistently growing in Christ-likeness.

As we saw in 2 Corinthians 3:18, we "are being transformed into the same image from glory to glory." This happens bit by bit, degree by degree.

Think about the church activities you participate in on a weekly basis. How many of them help you and others increasingly reflect the character of God? How?

Can you think of a fellow church member who is consistently growing in Christ-likeness? How could you learn from that person's life?

**... as His Character has been Revealed in His Word.**

Where do we go to learn about God's character? We go to God's Word. From beginning to end, Scripture reveals God's character to us.

Read Isaiah 6:1-7. What does this passage reveal about God's character?

How does Isaiah respond to this revelation of God's character? Can you identify with that response?

Holiness is the quality of being set apart from sin and totally devoted to God. How should holiness be displayed in the church? What does it look like in action?

Think of three concrete ways you can help your church grow in imaging the holiness of God, and write them below. Pray that God would enable you to take some of these steps this week.

1

2

3

As we've seen, a healthy church is a congregation that increasingly reflects God's character as His character has been revealed in His Word. Whatever else a church might be, it should be a mirror that displays the splendor of God's character.

# 3

# The Two-Step Plan to a Healthier Church

Most people have a pretty good idea about what to do to improve their physical health:

- Sleep: Get your eight hours.
- Diet: More fruits and veggies, fewer fats and sweets.
- Exercise: Get your heart rate up for over half an hour several times per week.

Becoming healthier sounds simple enough, although of course it's easier said than done. If sleep, diet, and exercise are how we can improve our physical health, what about our churches' health?

How do you think a church can become healthier?

Would you say that your church is growing healthier? Why or why not?

In yesterday's study we learned that a healthy church is a congregation that increasingly reflects God's character as His character has been revealed in His Word. How then does a church grow in reflecting God's character?

The answer is simple: By listening to and following God's Word. At the most basic level, the plan for a healthier church has only two steps: listen and follow.

A working mirror reflects the image in front of it because it takes it in and presents it back just as it really appears. So also our churches need to take in God's Word and then re-present it in our lives together.

**Step One: Listen**
We need to listen to God's Word because God's Word is the very source of the church's life.

Read Romans 10:17. According to this passage, how does faith come?

Read 1 Peter 1:23. What is it that has given us new birth?

According to Romans 10, we're saved through faith, and that faith only comes through hearing the Word of God. Or again, Peter reminds us we were born again, "not of perishable seed but of imperishable—through the living and enduring word of God" (1 Pet. 1:23).

The church's life comes through the Word of God. Further, we need to listen to God's Word because it is the source of the church's growth.

Read Acts 20:32. What, according to Paul, is the message of God's grace able to do? How should this impact how we try to grow as Christians?

In light of these passages, why is it important that churches devote themselves to listening to God's Word?

What do you think would happen to a church that failed to diligently and regularly listen to God's Word? Have you ever known a church like this?

What are some ways in which you regularly listen to God's Word? What impact does that listening have on you?

**Step Two: Follow**

The point of listening to God's Word is not simply to hear it, but to do it. James says that a man who listens to God's Word but doesn't put it into practice is like a man who looks at his face in the mirror and then immediately goes away and forgets what he looks like (Jas. 1:22-25). The point is not simply to listen, but to obey.

Read Matthew 7:24-27. What are the two options Jesus puts before us? What distinguishes the wise man from the foolish man?

How does Jesus' teaching in this passage relate to James 1:22-25?

In this stark word picture Jesus puts opposite alternatives before us: Either we build our lives on His words, or we don't. Jesus is teaching that mere hearing is not enough. The person who weathers the storm is the one who hears Jesus' words *and does them.*

What are some ways churches might be tempted to listen to God's Word but not follow it?

What are some things that might distract a church from devoting itself to listening to and following God's Word?

How can you help others in your church to listen to and follow God's Word?

Want a healthy church? Make sure you give it a steady diet of God's Word and a regular exercise regimen of living it out.

4

# The Most Important Thing About a Church

Sometimes it seems like everyone has an opinion about what's most important in church, and no two of those opinions are the same:

- For some people, it's having a good Sunday School class.
- For others, it's the youth group.
- For others, it's the missions emphasis week.
- For others, it's the food pantry.
- For still others, it's making sure the church sings the "right" style of music.

What do you think is most important in church? Why?

In the past few days, we've considered that a healthy church is a congregation that increasingly reflects God's character as His character has been revealed in His Word. And we've seen that in order to grow healthier, churches must listen to and follow God's Word.

Therefore, the most important thing a church must do is expose its people to God's Word every week, and the most effective way that the Word of God is "rerevealed" to God's people is through expositional preaching.

### What is Expositional Preaching?

Expositional preaching is simply preaching that *exposes* God's Word. It's preaching that rereveals God's Word to God's people. It takes a passage of Scripture, explains it, and then applies the meaning of the passage to the life of the congregation. More specifically, expositional preaching makes the main point of the biblical text the *main point* of the sermon.

An expositional sermon is *not*:

- Simply a running commentary on a passage;
- A sermon which focuses on a secondary topic in a given passage;
- Any sermon which appeals to Scripture for support.

Rather, an expositional sermon asks, "Why exactly did God inspire the author to write this? What exactly does it say? And how does it apply to the life of the church?" And it makes the answer to those questions the substance of the sermon.

Expositional preaching isn't the only kind of preaching a pastor may do, but it should be the church's main diet.

Read 2 Timothy 3:16-17. What does this passage teach about the nature and power of Scripture?

Read 2 Timothy 4:1-5. What challenges will Timothy face in his preaching ministry? How might these same things tempt preachers not to preach expositionally today?

Because all Scripture is inspired by God and profitable for growing the church in godliness (2 Tim. 3:16-17), pastors are called to preach the Word as their highest priority in ministry (2 Tim. 4:2). In view of these Scriptures, how would you respond to someone who says that preaching isn't important for the church and that we shouldn't bother with it anymore?

### Why Expositional Preaching is of First Importance

Maybe you're reading along and thinking, *I see why preaching matters, but the most important thing? Really? Aren't there dozens of other things that are just as important, if not more important?*

To understand why preaching God's Word is the most important thing about a church, try to imagine growing crops with no sunlight. You might have thousands of dollars worth of equipment. You might spend countless hours planning, plowing, and sowing seed. You might diligently water your crops every day. But with no sunlight, they simply won't grow. There won't be any life created. You'll have a lot of effort, but no fruit—or vegetables.

Without God's Word rerevealed through preaching, the church would be the same. The preached Word is what brings faith (Rom. 10:17). It's what calls sinners from death to life (1 Pet. 1:23). It's what builds up the church in love and holiness.

The preached Word is the match that lights the church's fire of good deeds. It's the electricity which powers a thousand other godly activities.

Everything else in a church's life flows from its preaching. If Sunday after Sunday God's revelation is rerevealed, His people will be conformed to His character. They will grow to love what He loves and hate what He hates. They will, increasingly, act the way He does. And that will spill over into countless practical efforts to carry out the teachings of God's Word. Preaching is what drives, directs, enables, empowers, and motivates those efforts.

How do you usually measure how good a sermon is?

Think of a good sermon you've heard recently. How did your life change because of it?

Pause and pray for your pastor. Thank God for his preaching. Pray that his preaching every week would be a faithful rerevelation of God's Word.

Expositional preaching is the most important thing a church can do, because it's as we listen to and obey God's Word that we grow in reflecting God's character.

# 5

# Listen Up!

Most of us probably haven't given much thought to how we listen to sermons.

You probably don't give much thought to how you brush your teeth or park your car either. They're just things you do on a regular basis. For many of us, listening to sermons is similar: we show up, sit in the pews, maybe daydream, maybe take notes, go home, and don't give it a second thought.

How do you listen to sermons? Do you have any regular habits or strategies for getting the most out of it?

What are some challenges to listening well to sermons? List as many as you can think of below.

How we listen to sermons matters. The way we listen reveals something about what we believe about God's Word and the preaching of it. God expects us to listen to and obey his Word. And one of the primary ways we receive that Word is through the preaching we hear in church every week.

So in this study we're going to consider how we should listen to sermons.

## Consider What You Want to Hear

Read 2 Timothy 4:3-4. What were these people listening for? What did they want to hear?

What do you want to hear when you listen to a sermon?

The people Paul wrote of in 2 Timothy 4 had gone astray because they didn't want to hear God's Word, but rather whatever fit their own passions. They didn't want to hear the truth God had revealed, but instead the smooth stories that justified the way they wanted to live. So consider carefully what you want to hear.

Evaluate how you usually listen to sermons right now. What does the way you listen reveal about what you are hoping to hear?

### Consider Scripture's Authority—and Receive the Preached Word Eagerly

Read Acts 17:10-11. In which two ways did Luke commend the Bereans?

1

2

Give some practical examples of what it looks like to receive the Word with all eagerness. How could you tell if someone was receiving a sermon eagerly?

The Bereans were commended for searching the Scripture to test whether the apostles' teaching lined up with it. What are some practical ways you can imitate this as you listen to your pastor's preaching?

The Bereans had a balanced attitude toward the teaching they heard. On the one hand, they received the apostles' teaching eagerly—they didn't listen with suspicion and skepticism. On the other hand, they diligently studied the Scriptures on their own to confirm that the teaching they heard was true. So consider Scripture's authority—and receive the preached Word eagerly.

### Listen in Order to Do

One of the greatest temptations we face in listening to sermons is to hear without doing. As we considered a few days ago, James warns us that a man who listens to the word but doesn't do it is like a man who looks in the mirror and then immediately forgets what he looks like (Jas. 1:22-25). What's the point of looking in the mirror if you pay so little attention that you immediately forget what you saw? Similarly, what's the point of listening to a sermon if you don't do what the Word tells you to do?

Jesus emphasized that what matters is hearing and *obeying* God's Word. In John 13:17 he says, "If you know these things, you are blessed if you do them." And in Luke 11:28, in response to someone blessing his mother, Jesus said,

***"Those who hear the word of God and keep it are blessed!"***

Are you tempted to hear the Word but not obey it? How so? Give specific examples.

What are some habits you can cultivate to help you hear the Word and obey it? Suggestion: Ask a godly, mature fellow church member how they try to live out what they hear. See if you might be able to imitate some of what they do.

As we've seen in our studies throughout this week, hearing the Word of God and living it out are the church's most fundamental callings. So consider how you listen to sermons. Listen eagerly. Consider the authority of Scripture. Consider what you want to hear—and whether what you want to hear is what God has to say. And listen, by God's grace, in order to *do*.

# 2

# The Truths on which Churches Build:

## *Biblical Theology and the Gospel*

## Getting Started

**Welcome back to your small-group discussion of *Church Essentials.* Begin your group by reflecting on the previous week's study.**

1 What are some things from this week's study that you'd like to discuss further or raise questions about?

2 What one truth sticks out to you from the study this week? What practical changes do you think God is calling you to make based on this study?

3 Look back to the study for Day 1. What are the two reasons why the church should be central in the Christian life?

4 According to this week's study, what is a healthy church?

5 How does a church grow healthier?

6 What do you think about the idea that rerevealing God's Word through expositional preaching is the most important thing a church does? Do you agree or disagree? Do you think this is an important point?

## View DVD Segment

**Watch the segment from the DVD using the viewer guide below.**

Theology is the KNOWLEDGE of God.

The Bible tells us the truth about what GOD is like, what we are like, and most especially about Jesus Christ.

The central message of the Bible is JESUS CHRIST.

Throughout history God has been sovereignly drawing the minds of His people to the THEMES of the gospel.

Jesus is our example, but more importantly, He is our SUBSTITUTE.

Every other religion is a religion of "do." Christianity alone is the religion of "DONE."

We like the idea of God OWING us something.

**Video sessions are available for purchase at lifeway.com/9marks**

## Group Response

**Discuss the segment with your group using the questions below.**

1. What reasons does Mark Dever give for why theology matters? Can you think of more?

2. Have you ever thought about the Bible as one big story from Genesis to Revelation? How does understanding the Bible as a single narrative help us make sense of the individual parts?

3. Do you think a pastor should preach the gospel in every sermon? Why or why not?

4. How would you summarize the gospel in one minute?

5. What are some corruptions or challenges to the gospel today? What impact are these having on churches?

**Close with prayer.**

# Session Two

## The Truths on which Churches Build

If you read the Bible, *how* do you read the Bible? Do you simply drop it on the floor and let it open to whatever page it happens to and read from there? Do you read it systematically, from beginning to end? Do you tend to focus on your favorite passages to the neglect of others?

Healthy churches not only teach the Bible, they teach the Bible soundly. Now sound is an old-fashioned word, but it basically means *reliable, accurate,* or *faithful*. At root, it is an image from the medical world meaning *whole* or *healthy*. A healthy church teaches the Bible soundly—it is faithful to the teaching of the entire Bible. It reliably and accurately interprets the parts in terms of the whole.

How does a church do that? And how do church members embrace it? They do so by understanding the entire message of the Bible and letting that message be the driving force in their understanding of God and their lives.

# 1
# Listening to the God who Speaks

Theology might sound intimidating, but it's really just the study of who God is. In fact, everyone who thinks about God is engaged in theology, whether they know it or not. But theology has fallen on hard times lately. Here are some objections to it you may have heard:

- If Christians can't agree on all the details of theology, why should we even bother?
- Doctrine divides, mission unites!
- Studying theology just wastes time that we could spend telling people about Jesus.
- Theology only puffs people up with pride. Jesus commanded us to love one another, not correct each other's doctrine.

What are some other objections to theology that you've heard?

Do you agree with these objections? Why or why not?

Despite its many detractors, theology plays a necessary and crucial role in the Christian life and in the life of the church. Why? Because God is a God who speaks.

## God Spoke Creation into Existence

Look up Genesis 1:3, 1:5, 1:9, 1:11, 1:14, 1:20, 1:24, and 1:26, Psalm 33:6 and 33:9, and Hebrews 11:3. What do these passages reveal about the nature of God's words?

As we see in these passages, God spoke creation into existence. This shows us that God's word is incomparably powerful. It brought worlds into existence out of nothing! God didn't need tools or electricity or even matter itself—He created all things simply by speaking.

## God Speaks His People into Existence

Look up Genesis 12:1-3. How did God bring Abraham into a special relationship with himself?

Look up Ezekiel 37:1-11. How, in this prophetic vision, does God resurrect his people from the dead?

What do both of these passages teach us about how God works by His Word?

As we see in these two passages, God calls His people to Himself and creates them anew through His Word. Just as He spoke the world into existence, God speaks His people into existence.

## God Reveals Himself through Speaking

Read Exodus 33:18-19 and 34:6-7. How does God reveal himself to Moses?

Why is it important to recognize that God reveals Himself through speaking? What will we miss about God if we don't realize this?

God not only creates and calls His people by His Word, He also reveals Himself by His Word. Just as our own speech reveals our character, desires, plans, and so on, so also God's speech reveals all those things about Him. And we know from 2 Timothy 3:16-17 that all of Scripture is breathed out by God—every word of the Bible is *spoken* by Him—so that all of it reveals God to us.

**Listening to the God who Speaks**

And when God speaks, we better listen. It is critical, of course, that we *do* what God tells us to do, but how do when know what He tells us to do? By listening to what He has said.

Further, being a Christian is not just about performing certain actions. It's first and foremost trusting in a person (Jesus), who is presented to us as Savior through a message (the gospel). The first step in the Christian life—whether we're just beginning or have been walking with Christ for fifty years—is always to listen to what God has said in His Word. Only then will we rightly know Him, love Him, worship Him, and follow Him.

This is the most basic reason why theology matters. God has revealed Himself to us richly in His Word. He has told us glorious and amazing things about who He is and what He has done for us in Christ. Theology is simply the discipline of carefully listening to and reflecting on what God has said, in order that we might respond rightly in our lives.

Have you ever thought about the wonderful truth that God has spoken to us in His Word? How should that simple fact affect your life? List as many concrete examples as you can think of.

If theology is simply listening to the God who speaks, how would you respond to the objections to theology that we considered at the beginning of the study?

What is one way that you can work to grow in your knowledge of God? Pray that God would enable you to take practical steps in it this week.

God has revealed Himself to us in His Word. So devote yourself, together with your whole church, to listening to the God who speaks.

# 2

# The Lifeblood of the Church

Most people think of theology as something for libraries and classrooms, associating it with stacks of books, long lectures, and confusing Latin terms. While all of these things have their place, theology belongs not just in libraries and classrooms but also in the church.

Not only that, but theology shouldn't be a mere sideshow in the church, limited to an occasional seminar or lecture, like a special add-on for the intellectual types. Rather, it should be the very lifeblood of the church.

## Theology is for Life

Yesterday we saw that theology is the discipline of listening to and reflecting carefully on what God has spoken in His Word. And, as we noted then, the point of theology is never *mere* listening.

Think about what we studied last week: in order to grow healthier, the church must listen to and follow God's Word. Theology, then, is not just a sheet of facts, but a set of marching orders. Theology isn't mere information, it's the script for living the Christian life.

In other words, theology is for life.

Look up Romans 12:1-2. Paul appeals to the Romans to present themselves as living sacrifices because of God's mercies. What do "the mercies of God" refer to? (Hint: Paul has spent a long time talking about them so far in Romans!)

What does this passage teach us about the relationship between theology and Christian living?

Most of Paul's letters follow this pattern of expounding the doctrines of the gospel and then calling Christians to live in light of those truths. Take the Book of Ephesians as one example. Ephesians 1-3 is about the greatness of Jesus and how in His greatness He has blessed us in the heavenlies with every spiritual blessing. Ephesians 4-6 is about how those truths are lived out. You can find a similar pattern in Paul's other letters.

Not only that, but within "application" sections of their writing, the New Testament authors are constantly appealing to theology in order to instruct Christians about how to live.

Look up Ephesians 5:1-2. What reasons does Paul give for why we should be imitators of God and should walk in love?

Theology is for life. Doctrine is for doing. Truth is for transformation. The one-two step of "listen and follow" should characterize every Christian and every church.

**The Lifeblood of the Church**

This means that theology, far from being a side-show for brainy types, should be the lifeblood of the church.

Read Titus 1:9-10. What does Paul say an elder (pastor) must be able to do? Why?

Read Titus 3:4-8. What are the things which Paul tells Titus to insist on? For what purpose (v. 8)?

Explain in your own words why it is important that churches consistently preach and teach sound doctrine. (Hint: Think of what will happen in these churches if they do or don't preach sound doctrine.)

Sound doctrine should be the bread and butter of a church's teaching ministry.

As a pastor preaches through portions of Scripture, he should carefully connect those passages to the bigger picture of what God has revealed in His Word. He should note what each passage teaches about who God is and what He has done for us in Christ.

And other teaching contexts, such as Sunday School or small groups, should similarly have the life-giving power of sound doctrine running through their veins.

Read Colossians 3:16-17. By what means are we to have the message of Jesus dwell in us richly? What does it mean for the message of Christ to dwell in us through the songs we sing as a church? What does that tell us about what those songs should be like?

Who, according to this passage, is to teach and admonish others in the church? Is it just pastors and other leaders?

What are some ways that you can teach and admonish others with sound doctrine? Pick one and ask God to help you do it this week.

As we see in this passage, the church's corporate worship should be filled with sound doctrine. We should be able to say that, through the songs we sing in church, the Word of Christ is dwelling richly in us.

Further, we are to come together not merely to worship God, but also to build each other up. How? By teaching the truth to each other. We do this through formal avenues like Bible studies and small groups, but we also do it through the songs we sing and the conversations we have. Theology should also spill over into all our interactions in the rest of the week. After all, it's as we speak the truth in love to one another that we all grow up into maturity in Christ (Eph. 4:16).

Sound theology should be the lifeblood of every church, because theology is for life.

# 3

# The Greatest Story that Ever Happened

The Bible can sometimes seem more than a little confusing. It contains poetry and proverbs, case law and covenants, history and heavenly visions. Its events take place on three continents over thousands of years, and it often features people with strange names who sometimes do even stranger things.

Does Scripture ever seem confusing or disorienting to you? Why? What parts in particular?

Are there any ways you've found to make sense of the whole Bible? What are they?

It's understandable that Scripture can seem disorienting at times, but have you ever considered that from beginning to end, the Bible tells a single story?

It begins with creation in Genesis 1, and it culminates in Revelation 21-22 with a new creation. Things start out good—very good actually (Gen. 1:31)—but soon go terribly wrong (Gen. 3). And the whole rest of the Bible is the story of how God, through Jesus, makes everything right again.

This story is not just the greatest story ever told, it's the greatest story that ever happened.

It's not always easy to see how each individual portion of Scripture fits into that big story, but it all does. And all of it, in one way or another, sheds light on the hero of the story: Jesus (John 5:39).

The Bible doesn't read like a novel, a single running narrative. But when we read from Genesis to Revelation with the life, death, and resurrection of Jesus as the focal point, we see that the whole thing hangs together as one epic story.

How do you think reading the Bible as one story would help you to make sense of confusing parts?

### A 30,000 Foot View of the Whole Bible

In order to see how the whole Bible fits together as one story, let's take a supersonic trans-canonical flight to see the whole thing from 30,000 feet:

- The **historical books** of the Old Testament begin at the beginning, when God created the entire universe. They then tell how humanity sinned against God, how God enacted a plan to bless all the nations through Israel, the special people He chose, and how Israel's sin earned God's judgment.
- The **wisdom literature** of the Old Testament teaches us how to rightly relate to God and live in a world broken by sin but brightened by God's promises.
- The **prophets** of the Old Testament convict God's people of sin and point forward to the day when God would restore His people's fortunes and extend salvation to the nations through His chosen Servant.
- Then, when we arrive at the New Testament, the **Gospels** show us how Jesus fulfilled these prophetic expectations and earned salvation for His people. This was realized through his sin-bearing death on the cross and his victory over death in his resurrection. The Gospels present to us both the teaching and example of Jesus so we would be able to follow Him rightly as His disciples.
- **Acts** tells the story of the earlier years of the spread of this good news of salvation in Jesus and the growth of the church.
- The **epistles** teach Christians and churches how to live in light of the gospel in a world that opposes Christ.
- And **Revelation**, like the prophetic books of the Old Testament, points forward to the time when God will perfectly bring His kingdom to earth, deliver His people from all sin and harm, and judge the wicked.

This, in a nutshell, is the greatest story that has ever happened. This is the story that the whole Bible tells and into which every book in the Bible fits. This story begins at the very beginning of the universe and stretches on into the future when God will fulfill all His saving promises and bring heaven to earth.

Scan through two biblical retellings of major portions of the Bible's story in Acts 7:2-53 and Acts 13:16-47. In different ways, these two speeches by early Christians summarize some of the main points of the entire biblical story. Would you retell the story of the Bible in this way? Why or why not?

### What Difference Does the Story Make?

The fact that the Bible tells one coherent story makes all the difference for how we interpret it and apply it to our lives.

Read Luke 24:25-27, Luke 24:47, John 5:39, and 2 Corinthians 1:20. How should these passages affect the way we read the whole story of Scripture?

How should they impact the way we approach any individual passage of Scripture?

Seeing the Bible as a single story means we come to understand that the Bible has one main point: to witness to God's saving work in Christ and to bring us to participate in it. That doesn't mean that it's the only thing the Bible does, but it does mean that the Bible is primarily about God's saving work in Christ.

Therefore, even though Scripture contains plenty of commands and comforts, we shouldn't view the Bible as simply a divine rule book or a treasury of comforting verses. Rather, we should understand Scripture fundamentally as the story of how Jesus rescues us from sin and death.

### Living Inside the Bible's Story

The story of the Bible starts long before we were born, and it continues long into the future—into eternity, in fact. Not only that, but we all live *within* the Bible's story.

The future the Bible promises is *our* future. History recorded in the Bible explains why things are the way they are here and now, even in our lives. God's plan of salvation that we see on the pages of Scripture is the same plan that's at work in our lives, our churches, and our communities.

How does seeing yourself within the biblical story change the way you think about:

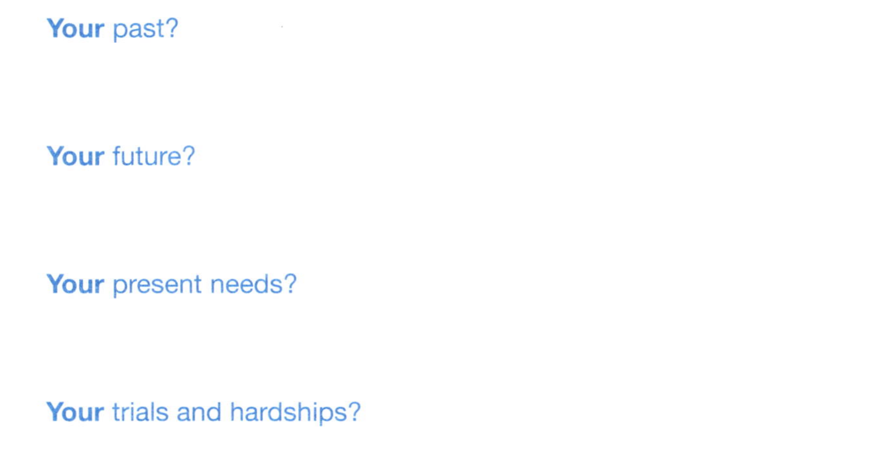

**Your** past?

**Your** future?

**Your** present needs?

**Your** trials and hardships?

Imagine a Christian friend coming to you feeling discouraged and overwhelmed by a struggle with sin. Describe how you would counsel them by applying the Bible's story to their struggle. (Hint: Remember to remind them that they live *within* this story!)

From Genesis to Revelation, from creation to new creation, the Bible tells the amazing story of how, through the Lord Jesus Christ, God saves us from sin and from *all* its effects. Praise God that this story is not only great, but true.

# 4

# The Best News Ever Told

What's a good piece of news you've heard recently? What made it so good?

From newspapers to Internet headlines, from TV in the evening to catching up with a friend, we tend to take in lots of news every day. Some of it's great news and some of it's terrible, but most of it is somewhere in the middle.

Yesterday we considered that the Bible presents one overarching story. Today we're going to push that one step further and see that at the heart of this story is a piece of good news—and it's the best news ever told.

This news, of course, is the gospel. (The Greek word from which we get the word *gospel* simply means *good news.*) So let's consider what makes this news so good, and why it's important that we know it by heart.

In your own words, what is the gospel?

## Gospel Confusion

Unfortunately, today there is much confusion among professing Christians about what the gospel is.

- Some people say it's simply a message telling us we need to live better lives.
- Some people say it's God wanting to be our friend.
- Some people say it's God wanting us to be happy, healthy, and rich in this life.
- Some people say it's God wanting to transform the world through us.

Why do you think there is so much confusion about what the gospel is?

Why do you think it's important that Christians get the gospel right?

## High-Definition Gospel

Thankfully, we're not left to ourselves to try to figure out what the good news is. God has told it to us in Scripture, and there are even a few places that provide a clear, compact summary of the gospel. One of those places is located in 1 Corinthians 15:1-4.

Look up 1 Corinthians 15:1-4. What does this passage teach about:

Our problem before God?

What Christ accomplished on the cross?

How we should respond to Christ's work?

How would you summarize this passage's teaching about the gospel in a couple sentences?

According to 1 Corinthians 15:1-4, the gospel begins with the bad news that we need saving from our sins. Because God is holy, and all human beings are sinful, His wrath is justly directed against us. But Jesus died for our sins (v. 3), bearing the punishment we deserved. And He rose from the dead (v. 4), conquering death for us. Now we must turn from our sin and trust in Christ—receiving this message from the heart and holding fast to it (vv. 1-2)—in order to be saved.

Based on this passage and others like it, we can sum up the gospel under four main headings: God, Man, Christ, Response.

1. **God**. God is the creator of all things (Gen. 1:1). He is perfectly holy, worthy of all worship, and will punish sin (1 John 1:5; Rev. 4:11; Rom. 2:5-8).
2. **Man**. All people, though created good, have become sinful by nature (Gen. 1:26-28; Ps. 51:5; Rom. 3:23). From birth, all people are alienated from God, hostile to God, and subject to the wrath of God (Eph. 2:1-3).
3. **Christ**. Jesus Christ, who is fully God and fully man, lived a sinless life, died on the cross to bear God's wrath in the place of all who would believe in Him, and rose from the grave in order to give His people

eternal life (John 1:1; 1 Tim. 2:5; Heb. 7:26; Rom. 3:21-26; 2 Cor. 5:21; 1 Cor. 15:20-22).

4 **Response**. God calls everyone everywhere to repent of his or her sins and trust in Christ in order to be saved (Mark 1:15; Acts 20:21; Rom. 10:9-10).

**Putting the Gospel to Work**

The implications of a right understanding of the gospel are nearly endless. In some ways, the whole Christian life is simply working out how we should live in light of what God has done for us in Christ. For now, we're going to consider just a few of those implications.

How do you deal with sin in your life? How does having a clear understanding of the gospel help you to rightly address your own sin?

How does a right understanding of the gospel affect how you interact with others' needs? What about others' sins?

One benefit of clearly understanding the gospel is that it equips you to share the gospel with others. So consider how you would share the gospel with a non-Christian friend and write a few sentences below try to cover all the bases without getting bogged down in unnecessary detail.

The gospel is the best news ever told. It's the headline for the Bible's entire story. And it sets the course for the entire Christian life. So study, meditate on, and share this news with others.

# 5

# Growing Gospel Fruit in the Church

Sometimes we treat the gospel as if it were just a ticket to get us into a right relationship with God. Once we're in, we throw away the ticket. It's served its purpose, and now we have no further use for it. However, as we began to see yesterday, the gospel has profound, ongoing implications for how we live as Christians.

Not only does the gospel tell us how to live as individuals—it's what defines the life of the whole church. So let's look at three fruits the gospel grows when it takes root in the life of the church.

## The Gospel Grows Forgiveness

Read Ephesians 4:32. What does Paul command us to do? What does he remind us of in order to motivate us to do this?

Have you ever struggled to forgive someone in the church? How should meditating on how God has forgiven you enable you to forgive others? (For further reflection, consider Jesus' parable in Matthew 18:21-35.)

One of the fruits the gospel grows in the church is forgiveness. When we remember that God has forgiven the massive debt of our sins, we learn how to forgive one another. This enables us to preserve love, unity, and harmony in the church that would otherwise be threatened by our sin.

## The Gospel Grows Unity

Read Philippians 2:1-11. What reasons does Paul give here for why we should humble ourselves for the sake of unity in the church?

Have you ever experienced unity in the church that crossed over boundaries of age, economics, or even past personal offenses? How was that unity achieved and preserved?

Why is unity important? What does the unity that's found in the gospel communicate about the gospel itself?

As we see in Philippians 2, the gospel grows unity. When we consider how Christ humbled himself for our ultimate good, we are moved to lay aside our personal preferences, agendas, desires, and goals, and to seek the good of others. When we remember that Christ counted our salvation more important than His very life, we learn to count others more important than ourselves, which builds and preserves unity.

Unity in the church comes when we forget about ourselves and seek the good of others, which is exactly what the gospel teaches us to do. After all, it's what Christ did for us.

## The Gospel Grows Generosity

Read 2 Corinthians 8:8-9. In this passage, Paul is asking the Corinthians to contribute financially to the needs of the poor saints in Jerusalem. What does he appeal to in order to motivate them to give?

How does Christ's willingness to become poor for our sake change the way you look at money?

How has the gospel inspired generosity in your own life? What about in the lives of others in your church?

The gospel teaches us that Christ sacrificed himself for our sake. He became poor that we might become rich. He lost all so that we might gain all. Thus, the gospel is what drives us to share material goods with those in need. We could consider many other fruits the gospel grows in the church, but the point is simple: The gospel isn't just a ticket into a relationship with God. And it doesn't just teach us how to live as individuals. Rather, the gospel is what powers the church's growth in conformity to the character of God.

What fuels a healthy church? Regular doses of the gospel, dug deep and planted in every area of the church's life.

### Constantly Planting Gospel Seeds in the Church

How then can the church experience these fruits of the gospel? By constantly planting gospel seeds. Consider the following ways the church should do this:

- **Preaching**. Pastors should preach the gospel every week, not only as a message to lost sinners, but as the means of helping the church grow in Christ.
- **Teaching**. Pastors and other teachers should constantly help every church member connect the dots between the gospel and the problems they face in life and in the church, whether that teaching occurs in Sunday School classes, small groups, or one-on-one.
- **Corporate Worship**. Jesus gave the church two visible signs of the gospel: baptism and the Lord's Supper. The church should use these ordinances as a means of reminding ourselves of the gospel, working it deeper into our hearts. Further, singing, prayers, and Scripture readings in our church services should all be grounded in the gospel and convey the power of the gospel.
- **Personal Discipling**. When we get together to encourage each other and spur each other on in Christ, in discipling or accountability relationships, we should not only challenge each other to take new actions for Christ. We should also constantly remind each other of the gospel and help each other to apply the gospel to sins, challenges, and struggles we face.

What are some ways you can help the gospel bear fruit in others' lives in your church? List as many as you can think of below. Pray that God would help you carry out one or two of these steps this week.

When the gospel takes root in our churches, it bears amazing fruit. Pray that God would bear that fruit in your church, for his glory.

# 3

# Connecting the Church's Inward Purity and Outward Witness:

## *Conversion and Evangelism*

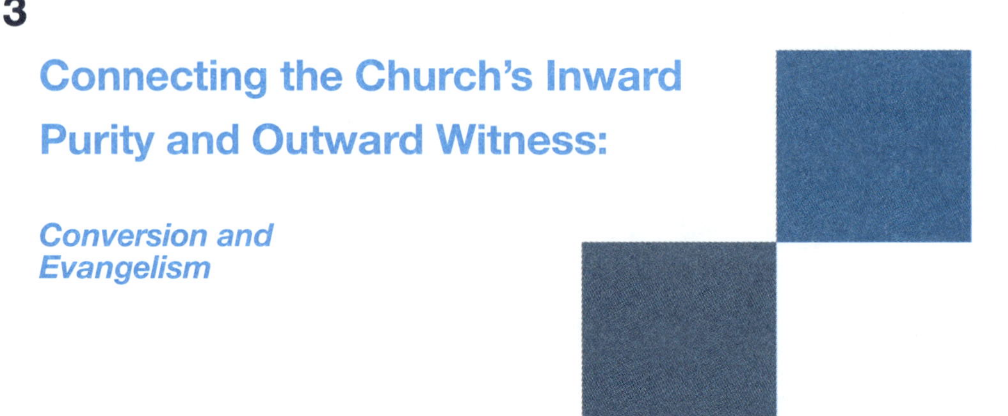

## Getting Started

**Welcome back to your small-group discussion of *Church Essentials.* Begin your group by reflecting on the previous week's study.**

1 What are some things from this week's study that you'd like to discuss further or raise questions about?

2 What one truth sticks out to you from the study this week? What practical changes do you think God is calling you to make based on this study?

3 Why is theology important? What role should it play in the church?

4 What does it mean to view yourself as living inside the story of the Bible? How does that change the way you consider your present circumstances?

5 What keeps you from sharing the gospel with others? How can you grow in evangelism?

6 Why is it important for the church to regularly rehearse the gospel? What are some of the fruits that the gospel grows in the church?

## View DVD Segment

**Watch the segment from the DVD using the viewer guide below.**

Jesus' _______________ program is the church.

You want to be in a church you're ____________ to bring non-Christians to.

We see more non-Christians scattered throughout the _________ than we can ever fit inside a church building.

The unpopular message of conversion is that everybody is __________ and needs to be changed.

If God is not ______________, we can't evangelize.

To repent you must first realize something is __________.

Repenting means recognizing what I've done is wrong and ____________ from that and trusting in God.

The _____________ of conversion is choosing the Savior over sin.

Evangelism makes clear that the message of what Christ has done is for _____________.

**Video sessions are available for purchase at lifeway.com/9marks**

## Group Response

**Discuss the segment with your group using the questions below.**

1. What are some wrong ideas about what it means to be a Christian? Where do these go wrong?

2. What does it mean to be a Christian?

3. How does someone become a Christian?

4. How does Mark Dever define evangelism? Do you agree with this definition? What does it mean for our lives as Christians and the life of the church?

5. Why is the church important for evangelism? How can the church help or hinder evangelistic efforts?

6. What are some ways that, as members of the same church, you can work together to evangelize your community? See if you can make specific plans to do so. Then pray and ask God to enable you to carry those plans out. And ask that he would bring people to Christ through your efforts.

**Close with prayer.**

# Session Three

## Connecting the Church's Inward Purity and Outward Witness

What does it mean to become a Christian? This is a key question for any church, for a healthy church is always pursuing the conversion of people to Christianity. A right understanding of conversion is not only the foundation for spiritual growth, but also the key to evangelism for any believer.

Understanding conversion rightly fuels evangelism, provides security, and emboldens courage built on the never-failing work of God. Or at least it does in healthy churches. The problem is that many Christians have difficulty in articulating what it means for them to be a Christian and are therefore paralyzed when it comes to sharing the gospel with another person.

Conversion isn't reciting a creed. It's not saying a prayer. It's not a conversation. It's not reaching a certain age, attending a class, or passing through some other rite of adulthood. It's not a journey, everyone strewn along the path at different points.

So what is conversion? Only by knowing the answer to that question can we rightly and passionately share the good news of Jesus Christ with others.

1

# Are You Sure You Know What a Christian Is?

People today have a lot of different ideas about what it means to be a Christian.

- Some think that they're born Christian, like they're born a Texan or with brown eyes.
- Some think that simply not being an atheist or a Muslim is enough to make you a Christian.
- Some think that a Christian is anyone who believes in God.
- Some think that anyone who's a nice person is a Christian.
- Some think that anyone who has prayed a certain prayer or walked down an aisle is a Christian.

Why do you think people have so many different ideas about what makes someone a Christian? What do you think makes someone a Christian?

**A Christian is ...**
According to Scripture, a Christian is someone who trusts in Jesus as Savior and Lord. This means that a Christian is someone who totally depends on Christ to save them from their sin, and who obediently submits to Christ's rule over their life.

### ... Someone who Trust in Jesus as Savior ...

Look up Acts 2:21, Acts 4:12, and Acts 16:31. According to these passages, how is someone saved?

Why do we need to be saved? Can someone be a Christian who doesn't think they need to be saved from anything?

If someone thinks Jesus is a good teacher and moral example, does that make them a Christian? Why or why not?

In order for someone to trust in Jesus as Savior, they must first come to understand their need of saving. This, in and of itself, is a work of God. Most people, especially those who live in an affluent society, don't think of themselves as being in danger. But the spiritual truth is that everyone ever born is in grave peril. Their souls are at stake because of sin, and it's from sin they must be delivered. We all need a Savior.

According to Acts 2, those who responded to Peter's message were baptized, joined the church, and began living a whole new way of life. They were publicly marked out as followers of Jesus. While they weren't yet called "Christians," these early believers demonstrate to us that it is those who trust in Jesus for salvation—and no others—who are Christians.

### … and Lord.

Just as often, the apostles proclaimed to people that Jesus is Lord and we must submit to Him.

Read Acts 2:36-38. What does Peter say about Jesus? What effect does this have on his hearers? What does Peter tell them to do in response?

Why does Jesus' Lordship require us to repent (that is, turn away from sin)?

Read Romans 10:9-10. What must we confess in order to be saved?

Do you think someone can be a Christian who does not submit to Jesus' Lordship and turn away from sin? Why or why not?

All throughout the New Testament, Jesus is proclaimed as Savior and Lord. He saves us from our sin, and He delivers us from its power. He provides forgiveness for sins, and He calls us to live a new life in submission to Him.

Because Jesus is Savior and Lord, we are called to the twin response of faith and repentance, which are really two sides of the same coin.

- In repentance we turn away from our former way of life. We cease to be our own masters and submit to Christ's rule.
- And in faith we turn to Christ and receive Him for all that He is.

## Proof of Faith: A Transformed Life

Perhaps the earliest name for Christianity was "the Way" (Acts 9:2). Why did the early believers call it "the Way"? Because from the earliest days of the church, Christians recognized that being a Christian was an entire way of life.

To be a Christian is to be a disciple, that is, a follower, of Jesus. Disciples are people who learn from, and imitate the practices of, their teacher. To be a Christian is more than simply living how Jesus lived, but it is never less.

Read John 8:31-32 and John 14:15. What does Jesus say will characterize His disciples?

Read Matthew 7:21-25. What does Jesus say about those who claim to believe in Him but don't obey his teachings? Are they really His followers?

Based on Jesus' teachings in these passages, do you believe there are people who think they are Christians but aren't? How might you minister to a person like that?

Of course Jesus doesn't expect us to obey His teachings perfectly. If we were able to do that, then why would we need a Savior to begin with? He knows that we will still struggle with sin, just as His first disciples did. But Jesus' point is that the test of whether anyone claims to believe in Him is whether or not they obey His teaching. We'll consider this more in tomorrow's study.

For now, the point is simple: to be a Christian means to trust in Jesus as Savior and Lord. And the proof of that faith is in following Jesus' commands.

# 2

# Are You Sure You're a Christian?

In our society, to question whether someone is really a Christian seems mean and judgmental. But Jesus clearly teaches that there will be people who think they are His followers but really aren't (Matt. 7:22-25). And being mistaken about this has eternal consequences.

Therefore, it's not surprising that Scripture actually commands us to examine whether or not we really are Christians. In 2 Corinthians 13:5 Paul writes,

> ***"Test yourselves to see if you are in the faith. Examine yourselves. Or do you yourselves not recognize that Jesus Christ is in you?—unless you fail the test."***

The Book of 1 John was written in order to help Christians know they are truly believers and have eternal life (1 John 5:13). By studying some verses from this book, we can begin to perform the kind of self-analysis Paul commands.

First John lays out two primary tests to separate a true believer from a false one.

### Test #1: Belief

Read 1 John 4:15. What is true of the person who confesses that Jesus is the Son of God?

Read 1 John 5:1. What is true of the person who believes that Jesus is the Christ?

Based on these two passages, what would you say it is necessary to believe in order to be a Christian?

Do you believe that Jesus is the Christ and the Son of God?

According to 1 John, one must believe that Jesus is the Messiah—God's anointed Savior-King—and the Son of God in order to truly be a Christian.

This belief is not mere head knowledge, like believing a news story you heard this morning is true. Rather, this belief involves conviction of the truth and trust in the person of Christ.

### Test #2: Life

Read 1 John 3:1-10. What does John say about the person who keeps on sinning (v. 6)?

What does John say about the person who abides in Jesus (v. 6) and has been born of God (v. 9)?

According to verse 10, how can we know the difference between the children of God and the children of the Devil?

How would you summarize John's teaching in this passage about how to tell a true Christian from a false one? What test does he hold up?

Do you consistently obey God's commands? What's the evidence of that in your life?

John's basic teaching in this passage is that those who are born of God obey God's commandments. Later in his letter, he specifies that one of the main commandments Jesus has given is that we love one another, just as God in Christ has already loved us (John 3:11-18; 4:7-21).

Test 1 and Test 2 are really two sides of the same coin. Those who truly trust in Jesus as Savior and Lord will live in a way that demonstrates that belief. They will practice what they believe.

**Patterns, not Perfection**

Many genuine believers work through passages like these and feel they can't possibly be Christians because they still struggle with sin. After all, doesn't John say that no one who abides in him keeps on sinning (1 John 3:6)?

Read 1 John 1:8-10. What does John say about the person who claims to have no sin?

What does John say God does when we confess our sin (v. 9)?

Does John expect that believers will obey God perfectly? Give evidence for your answer.

From this passage, it's clear that in other parts of the letter John is speaking about patterns, not perfection. He's speaking about our general course of life, not requiring that someone obey Christ perfectly in order to be a Christian. His point in 3:6 is that no one who is truly in Christ continues in the habitual practice of sin.

To become a Christian, according to John, is to make a decisive break with sin. It's to throw off sin's mastery and submit to Jesus as Lord. It's to begin to love God and love His people.

So, a true Christian is someone who believes in Jesus as Savior and Lord, and whose life shows evidence of that belief. As Jesus said,

***"If you love me, you will obey my commands" (John 14:15).***

How do you fare in John's two tests? Do they raise any questions about your faith?

Do you know anyone who claims to be a Christian but their beliefs or life don't seem to match the New Testament's definition of a Christian? How might you minister to that person?

God doesn't mean for us to consider these questions alone. After all, the command to examine yourself (2 Cor. 13:5) was addressed to the whole church. However you fare in John's tests, talk to others in your church about these matters.

God has given us the church to help us discern the fruit of faith in our life. Fellow believers will often be more accurate judges of our lives than we are. They can spot the fruit of faith when we might only see failure. So talk to a trusted fellow church member about these matters. It could do good to both of your souls.

# 3

# Christians Aren't Born—They're Made

No one comes out of the womb a Christian. That means for every believer, there was a time before we were in Christ. Not all of us can pinpoint exactly when we became a Christian, and that's OK. But the point is that Christians are not born, they're made.

The question then is, "How is a Christian made?" According to Jesus, a Christian is made not by being born, but by being "born again."

## By God

First, a Christian is made by God.

Read John 3:1-8. How is a person born again? Who gives this new birth?

Read John 1:12-13. How are the children of God spiritually "born"? Is it by our own effort or decision?

Read Ephesians 2:1-3. Before we were converted, what kind of spiritual shape were we in?

Read Ephesians 2:4-5. What did God do to us when we were dead in sin? Why did he do this (v. 4)?

The fundamental point in all these passages is the same: A Christian is made by God. Before our conversion, we were dead. Then, God made us alive. The fact that any of us are Christians is totally due to God's undeserved mercy, grace, and love.

## Through the Gospel

Read 1 Peter 1:23. Through what are we born again?

Read Romans 10:9-17. According to Paul, how is someone saved (vv. 9-10)? Can someone be saved without hearing the gospel (vv. 14-17)?

It's a simple point, but an important one: a Christian is made through the gospel. Only people who hear the gospel can be saved. God is the One who gives us the new birth, and He does it through the gospel.

## Our Response: Repent and Believe

God gives us new life through the gospel. But what response does this bring about in us?

Read Mark 1:15. What does Jesus tell us to do in response to His preaching of the good news? What do you think it means to repent?

Do you think someone can have true faith without repentance? What about repentance without faith? Do either of them make sense without the other?

How is a Christian made? Through the gospel, God gives life to a dead sinner, enabling him or her to repent of sin and trust in Christ. We see all this together in the case of Lydia in Acts 16. The apostles preached the gospel (v. 13), the Lord opened her heart to receive the message (v. 14), and Lydia repented, believed, and was baptized (v. 14).

This means that becoming a Christian doesn't necessarily involve walking an aisle, signing a card, or praying a set prayer. All those things can happen without a person truly repenting and believing. And a person can repent and believe without doing any of those things.

A Christian is someone who has responded to the gospel in repentance and faith. Of course that's not the end of the Christian life, but the beginning. A Christian should go on to be baptized, join a church, and begin living a whole new life empowered by the Holy Spirit.

God uses a diversity of means to convict people of sin and bring them to faith, but fundamentally all Christians are made the same way: God enables us to respond to the gospel with repentance and faith.

To repent simply means to turn. It means to renounce our previous way of life in which we loved sin and trusted in ourselves, our intellect, or our emotions for our salvation. We must turn from that and go a new way—the way of belief and trust in Christ alone.

How did you become a Christian?

Have you ever thought about the fact that it was God who enabled you to repent and believe? How should that impact your attitude toward God?

Is it possible for us to guarantee that someone we're sharing the gospel with will become a Christian? Why or why not?

It's because of God's grace and mercy alone that any of us are Christians. If it weren't for God causing us to be born again, we'd still be dead in our sins, and we would still reject Christ.

But now, those of us who believe in Christ have our sins forgiven, have new life in the Holy Spirit, and have the sure hope of eternal life with God. Praise the Lord for his powerful work in conversion!

# 4

# Evangelism 101: We Preach, God Works

Very few areas of the Christian life inspire more guilt than evangelism. In fact, its only rival in that respect is probably prayer!

There are lots of reasons why we don't evangelize, but one of them is simple: We don't really know what evangelism is.

How would you define evangelism in a couple sentences?

Do you struggle to evangelize? Why or why not?

## Evangelism Defined

Simply stated, evangelism is telling non-Christians the good news about what Jesus Christ has done to save sinners. This good news is that:

1. God is holy (1 John 1:5) and the creator of all things (Gen. 1:1).
2. All people are sinners who deserve God's righteous, eternal wrath (Rom. 3:10-19; Mark 9:48; Rev. 14:11).
3. Jesus Christ, who is fully God and fully man, lived a sinless life, died on the cross to bear God's wrath in the place of all who would believe in Him, and rose from the grave in order to give His people eternal life (John 1:1; 1 Tim. 2:5; Heb. 7:26; Rom. 3:21-26; 2 Cor. 5:21; 1 Cor. 15:20-22).
4. The only way to be saved from eternal punishment and be reconciled to God is to repent of sin and trust in Jesus Christ for salvation (Mark 1:15; Acts 20:21).

Evangelism is telling others this basic message. And because this message demands a response, we must urge people to repent and believe. Yet because only God can bring about that response, we must not manipulate people to respond in a way that may satisfy us, yet not be true repentance and faith.

## Examples of Evangelism

Read Acts 8:1-4. Who was scattered by the persecution (v. 1)? What did those who were scattered by persecution do (v. 4)?

Read Acts 8:26-40. What can we learn from Philip's example of evangelism?

As we see in the New Testament, all believers, not just the apostles or other church leaders, shared the good news about Christ with others. In Acts 8 we see Philip explaining the gospel from the Old Testament Scriptures, which teaches us, among other things, to use the Bible in our evangelism.

## Mandate to Evangelize

Read Matthew 28:16-20. What is the command Jesus gives his disciples in v. 19? What are the disciples to teach others to do (v. 20)?

Do you think this passage commands all Christians to share the gospel with others? Explain. (Hint: Does "everything I have commanded you" include the command he just gave them?)

In this passage, Jesus commanded His disciples to go and make more disciples. And He commanded the disciples to teach these new disciples to obey everything He commanded—which includes the command to make more disciples! Therefore, Jesus commands all Christians to go and share the good news with others, calling them to repent and believe in Christ.

Yet as we considered last week, God is the One who ultimately makes people Christians. God is the One who gives the gift of faith and repentance (Acts 11:18; Phil. 1:29). God is the One who causes dead sinners to be born again through the gospel (John 1:12-13; 3:1-8; 1 Pet. 1:23).

So there's a simple equation to evangelism: We preach, God works. We scatter seed, God makes it grow (Mark 4). We herald the good news, God brings people to repent and believe in it.

We can't predict how God will work, and we can't force people to respond. But we can always be confident that when we preach the gospel, God will work (Isa. 55:10-11).

How does distinguishing our role in evangelism (sharing the good news) from God's role (converting people) provide encouragement for evangelism?

What are some of the joys and blessings evangelism brings?

Think of three non-Christians in your life whom you have not evangelized. Write down their names. Pray that God would enable you to share the good news with all three. Write down a specific step you can take this week to share the gospel with one of them.

# 5

# The Church is God's Evangelism Program

We tend to think of evangelism as an individual matter. Parachurch workers canvass university campuses, meeting up with students one-on-one. Traveling evangelists crisscross the country preaching the good news. You and a handful of friends go share the gospel at the local park.

While all of these individual activities can be faithful ways to fulfill the Great Commission, God actually has a plan for evangelism that's bigger than any one of them, or even all of them put together.

The church is God's evangelism program.

The church is supposed to faithfully preach the gospel in its corporate assemblies. But God's evangelistic purposes for the church go beyond simply preaching the gospel, as crucial as that is.

## City on a Hill

Read Matthew 5:13-16. What does Jesus say will be the result of our good deeds shining before men?

Why would people give glory to God for what they see in us?

Sometimes we are tempted to conform to the ways of this world. Why, according to this passage, is it important for Christians to be different from the world?

Jesus wants the church to be like a city on a hill. He wants our holy lives to shine like bright lights in the midst of the darkness around us. And the result is that people will glorify God.

We see this pattern throughout the New Testament. The people of the church are called to live lives that are holy and set apart from the world so that we would adorn the gospel, like fine jewelry adorns a woman's appearance (Titus 2:10; 1 Pet. 2:11-12).

## A Display of the Gospel

Read John 13:34-35. How will all people know that we are Christ's disciples?

Sometimes people consider fellowship to be in opposition to evangelism, as if any attention we give to building relationships in the church is simply time taken away from sharing the gospel with non-Christians. How does Jesus' teaching here correct that?

Read John 17:20-21. What does Jesus pray for the church (v. 20)?

What result does Jesus envision when His prayer is fulfilled (v. 21)?

Why do you think the church's unity, in particular, has this evangelistic role?

In these passages from John's Gospel, Jesus teaches that the church is to be a display of the gospel. In the church's love for its own, the world should see a picture of God's love for His own. In the church's unity, the world should see a picture of the unity that exists between the Father and the Son.

The result of the latter, in particular, is that the world would come to accept that Jesus is who He says He is. Jesus' goal for the church's unity is that through it, people would come to faith in Him.

This is why the church is God's evangelism program. The church is to be a display of the gospel. When the world looks at our love for each other, they should see a reflection of God's love. When the world sees our unity—a unity amid all kinds of diversity—they should be driven to reflect on the power of the gospel and the unity that there is between the Father, Son, and Holy Spirit.

The point is that it's not just our lives that commend the gospel, it's our life together. It's not just our individual holiness, but the way we relate to one another, that broadcasts the power of the gospel to the world.

## The Church's Corporate Witness at Work

Do you know anyone who was drawn to Christ through seeing the corporate life of the church? What was it about the life of the church that commended the gospel to that person?

If the church is meant to be a display of the gospel, how should that affect the way we do evangelism?

How should it impact our life in the church? The way we approach relationships in the church? How we handle sin and disunity?

God's plan for the church is not only to preach the gospel but also to display it. The church is God's evangelism program.

4

# Guarding the Church's Front Door and Opening its Back:

## *Church Membership and Discipline*

# Getting Started

**Welcome back to your small-group discussion of *Church Essentials.* Begin your group by reflecting on the previous week's study.**

1 What are some things from this week's study that you'd like to discuss further or raise questions about?

2 What one truth sticks out to you from the study this week? What practical changes do you think God is calling you to make based on this study?

3 Did your understanding of what it means to be a Christian change at all through this week's study? If so, how?

4 If conversion is fundamentally God's work, how should that impact how we evangelize? Does it mean that we shouldn't call people to repent and believe?

5 What are some reasons you *don't* evangelize? How can you overcome those barriers?

6 How does your church collectively display the gospel? How can your church work together to display a clearer and more compelling picture of the gospel?

## View DVD Segment

**Watch the segment from the DVD using the viewer guide below.**

When you join a local church, you are committing yourself to something ____________ that God is doing.

Selfish, ____________, fallen—no commitment | Christian—__________________

Church leaders should expect church members to:

1 ______________ for them
2 Submit to their leadership
3 __________________

When we're in a church together, we have special ____________ for each other.

Part of the responsibility of church membership is to make sure we're not _______________ ourselves.

Jesus told us to join a local church because:

1 It's good for you __________________ as a Christian.
2 It's good for other Christians.
3 It's good for ___________________.
4 It's good for the leaders of the church.
5 It's for the ___________ of God.

Church discipline is both _______________ and corrective.

_____________________ is when the local church withdraws their endorsement of a person's confession of faith.

Christians are often scared of church discipline because they think it will __________ the church.

Church discipline reflects God's ___________, not His wrath.

To resist church discipline is to be ______________.

Church discipline reflects the ______________ of God.

The whole reason to have church membership is to ________________ each other follow Jesus.

**Video sessions are available for purchase at lifeway.com/9marks**

## Group Response

**Discuss the segment with your group using the questions below.**

1 According to Mark Dever, why should every Christian join a church? Do you agree with him? Why or why not?

2 How would you answer someone who said, "Membership is just a formality. You don't see it in the Bible. What counts is whether I'm involved in the people's lives by loving them and serving them"?

3 What kind of a difference do you think church membership makes to the Christian life? Give examples from your own life.

4 What is your initial response to the idea of church discipline? Do you think it's a good idea? Why or why not?

5 Have you ever been in a church that practiced church discipline? Why do you think that many churches don't practice church discipline?

6 What does Jesus teach about church discipline in Matthew 18:15-17? What does this mean for churches?

**Close with prayer.**

# Session Four

## Guarding the Church's Front Door and Opening its Back

A temple has bricks. A flock has sheep. A vine has branches. And a body has members. Being a Christian means being joined to a church.

Right? Is church membership a biblical idea? In one sense, no. Open up the New Testament, and you won't find a story about, say, Priscilla and Aquila moving to the city of Rome, checking out one church, then another, and finally deciding to join a third. From what we can tell, nobody went "church shopping" because there was only one church in each community. In that sense, you won't find a list of church members in the New Testament.

This argument, however, overlooks the fact church membership isn't explicitly stated in the New Testament because it was assumed. It was unthinkable for a person to be a Christian and not be a member of a church.

Church membership is a great joy and a tremendous responsibility. It means entrusting yourself to the care of leaders and listening to spiritual direction. Church membership, in a healthy church, is the boundary line between those who are in Christ and those who are not.

# 1
# Why Join a Church? Because it's Jesus' Embassy

You're probably a member of a number of organizations. Maybe a gym, a neighborhood association, a parent teacher group, or a sports team. Perhaps even a credit card rewards program.

You probably aren't required to belong to any of those things, yet you choose to because they bring you certain benefits or enable you to accomplish certain goals. And, if they stopped bringing those benefits or enabling those goals, you'd probably resign your membership with no questions asked and no hard feelings on either side.

In our society, this is how we tend to think of "membership."

So when we come to church membership, people tend to treat it the same way. If you want to obtain certain benefits (like the ability to vote in business meetings) or to accomplish certain goals (like being a church leader), then you join a church. If not, you don't. You may attend faithfully and serve devotedly, but never join the church because, well, what's the point?

Do you think church membership is an optional add-on to your life in the church? Why or why not?

Do you think there are any problems with treating the church like we might treat a neighborhood association, joining or resigning solely at our convenience?

What does your current attitude toward church membership show about your belief regarding the church itself?

For those who claim to follow Christ, joining a local church is not optional. Instead, it's actually how we express our submission to Jesus, our King.

## The Church is Jesus' Embassy

Have you ever been to a nation's embassy? It's an authorized institution which represents its home nation in a foreign country. In fact, when you step into an embassy, you are technically stepping onto the soil of that country, wherever in the world the embassy is located.

The church, as we're going to see, is Jesus' embassy. This has radical implications for the relationship between our claim to follow Christ and church membership.

Read Matthew 16:13-20. What does Peter confess about Jesus (v. 16)? What does Jesus say He will do in response to Peter's confession (v. 18)?

What does Jesus give to Peter in verse 19? With what result?

What we see in this passage is a grant of authority. Peter rightly confesses that Jesus is God's Messiah, the anointed Savior-King whom God promised to send to His people. And, in response, Jesus promises to build the church on Peter (and, implicitly, upon all who rightly confess Jesus as Messiah like Peter has). And He gives Peter the keys to the kingdom of heaven.

Read Matthew 18:15-18. What does Jesus say the church must do to a professing believer who persists in unrepentant sin (v. 17)?

What does Jesus say about the church's action in verse 18? How does this relate to what we see in Matthew 16:19?

In these verses, we have an application of Jesus' teaching from chapter 16.

In this passage, Jesus clarifies that it is the church as a whole that ultimately wields the keys to the kingdom of heaven. It is the church who determines to exclude an unrepentant sinner from its membership (18:17). And Jesus says of the whole church,

***"Whatever you bind on earth will be bound in heaven and whatever you loose on earth will be loosed in heaven" (Matt. 18:18).***

In other words, Jesus is saying that the church speaks for heaven. The church declares to the world who belongs to Jesus and who doesn't.

Does this reality bother you? Why or why not?

Is it possible for churches to abuse this authority? How?

When we put all this together, we see that the church is Jesus' embassy. The church declares the will of heaven on earth. It's the church that declares to the world who belongs to Jesus and who doesn't. In practice, of course, the church doesn't do this perfectly. But don't miss this: It is the church which has the authority to do so.

This means that one of the most basic ways we submit to Jesus is by submitting to the church.

Imagine you were just drafted to the NFL. The first thing the owner of your team says is, "Go report to the coach!" So also we as Christians are called to submit to the church—Jesus' authorized embassy of his heavenly kingdom—as an aspect of what it means to submit to Christ as Lord.

This makes sense out of the rest of the New Testament, where we see that:

- All those who believe the gospel are baptized and join the church (Acts 2:37-41).

- It is assumed that every Christian is also a member of a local church. Those who claim to follow Christ are inside the church, and those who don't are outside (1 Cor. 5:9-13).
- It is assumed that Christians have submitted to particular leaders (Heb. 13:17), and that they know who those leaders are, and the leaders know who they are.

Why should you join a church? Because Jesus has established the church as the only authorized embassy of His kingdom. And if you're a citizen of His kingdom, He calls you to submit to the authority He has established on earth for declaring His will and ways to the world.

How does viewing the church as an embassy change how you look at church membership? In this light, how is the church different from a neighborhood association or a credit card points program?

Are you a member of a church? Why or why not? If not, what do you plan to do about that in view of Jesus' teaching in these passages?

Have you ever considered that church membership involves submitting to the church, not just "joining" it? What difference does that make? Why is it important that we submit to the church?

## 2
# More than a Name on a List

One of the reasons some people don't join a church—or if they do, they don't give it much thought or weight—is that joining a church can feel like simply putting your name on a list.

Churches don't take roll and give you a grade at the end of the year, so if church membership is simply putting your name on a list, what's the point? What difference does it make?

Church membership is, and should be, far more than simply a name on a list.

### Membership Defines the Church

Read 1 Corinthians 5:9-13. Why does Paul give opposite instructions about how to relate to Christians and non-Christians who live in sin?

Membership isn't just a name on a list—it defines how we're to relate to people. Someone who is "inside" the church (1 Cor. 5:12) is expected to live as a Christian and should be held accountable by the church. Someone who is "outside" the church is assumed to be a non-Christian, and so we don't expect him or her to live like a Christian.

The first thing to see here is that Paul simply assumes that all Christians will be "inside" the church. He assumes that there won't be any of God's sheep simply hanging around outside the sheepfold.

Second, membership in the church carries serious implications for how we are expected to live, as well as how we should treat each other. Inside, people are expected to live like Christians, are under the authority of the church, and are held accountable to follow Jesus. Outside, none of those things are true.

Third, the church members *are* the church. Those who are members are "inside" the church, and those who are not members are outside. Church membership defines the shape and the boundaries of the church.

For Paul, membership is more than a name on a list—it defines the church. And it has radical implications for how we should live and relate to each other.

## Membership Defines the Christian Life

Read Hebrews 10:24-25. What does the author command us not to forsake? Instead, what should we do?

Based on this passage, what are some things that should characterize the life of every church member?

Why do you go to church? What reasons does this passage give for why we should go to church? What attitude should we have about going to church?

This passage commands us not to give up coming to church, but instead to keep on spurring each other on to love and good deeds. A Christian should meet with the church every week, and should regularly come up with ways to encourage fellow church members in their growth in Christ.

Read Colossians 3:12-17. List all the different instructions Paul gives us in this passage.

What do all of these commands (except the very last one in verse 17) have in common? What holds them together?

Pick one of these commands. Pray that God would grow you in living this out in your local church.

Colossians 3 contains many of the "one anothers" which fill the pages of the New Testament. But what we don't often consider is: who are we responsible to fulfill these "one anothers" with? Of course we should have a brotherly love toward all Christians everywhere, but it's tough to accept (v. 13), forgive (v. 13), and teach and admonish (v. 16) people you don't see regularly. Further, Paul wrote these commands to a local church, and the letter was to be read aloud to the whole church (Col. 4:16).

Put all this together and it's clear that the local church is the primary place for fulfilling these "one anothers." It is first and foremost our fellow church members whom we should be compassionate and kind to (v. 12), whom we should make peace with (v. 15), and whom we should build up through worshiping God together (v. 16).

In other words, your local church—the church you're a member of—should define the shape of your Christian life.

Do you tend to view church membership as simply putting your name on a list? In what specific ways has this study challenged that?

In light of these passages, how would you counsel a member of your church who hasn't been attending regularly and doesn't really see the point of participating in church?

Membership is more than a name on a list. It defines the church, and it defines the Christian life.

3

# The Pain and Purpose of Discipline

In order to think about discipline in the church, we're going to start by considering more broadly how discipline works in the Christian life. Right off the bat you might be thinking that discipline is something that just sounds painful—and it often is.

Think of someone who runs hundreds of miles over several months in order to train for a marathon. Or consider a student who fails a class because they got caught cheating on the final.

Both kinds of discipline are painful, but both have a positive purpose. The runner trains night and day to be able to accomplish the amazing feat of running 26.2 miles in one shot. The school authorities punish the student in order to maintain justice, and hopefully point the student toward the path of integrity.

Discipline may hurt, but it can bear good fruit—fruit that wouldn't come any other, easier way.

What are some disciplines you regularly exercise? What fruit have you seen from discipline in these areas?

What are some areas of life you struggle to be disciplined in? How does that lack of discipline impact your life?

## Discipline Yourself for the Purpose of Godliness

Read 1 Timothy 4:7-8. What does Paul command Timothy to do?

What reason does Paul give for why Timothy should discipline himself for the purpose of godliness?

Why do we need to discipline ourselves for godliness? Give other reasons from Scripture.

How have you experienced the benefits of discipline for the purpose of godliness? What growth has come in your life through grace-driven discipline?

Scripture commands us to discipline ourselves for the purpose of godliness. Why? Because godliness holds promise for both now and eternity.

But why do we need to discipline ourselves for godliness? Because we don't become more godly by accident.

Growing as a Christian isn't like floating down a river—it's more like swimming upstream against a surging current. The world tries to get us to live according to its ways, not Christ's ways. Our own flesh tempts us to indulge in sin. Growing in godliness, like running a marathon, takes constant effort. Ultimately, we grow through the power of the Holy Spirit, by God's grace, but that grace calls us to the disciplined pursuit of godliness (1 Cor. 15:10).

## God Disciplines Us for our Good, that We May Share His Holiness

Read Hebrews 12:3-11. What does God do to every son he loves (v. 6)?
For what purpose does God discipline us (vv. 10-11)?

How does discipline feel now (v. 11)? What fruit does it bring later (v. 11)?

These Christians were suffering for their faith. Because of that, they might have been tempted to doubt God's love and goodness. So the author of Hebrews reminds them that God was not angry with them. God hadn't turned His back on them. And their suffering wasn't because God simply looked the other way at the wrong time.

No, God allowed them to suffer to be made more holy. He was allowing them to experience the pain of suffering so that it would train them in holiness.

God disciplines us because He loves us. And He disciplines us for our good, that we may share His holiness.

What are some experiences you've had that you would consider God's discipline? How did it feel at the time? What fruit came from it later on?

When you experience hard things in life, are you tempted to doubt God's love or his goodness? Based on this passage, what do we know is true of God's character and of His attitude toward us, His children?

Based on this passage, how should we respond to trials?

Discipline for the purpose of godliness may be painful at present, but it will bear fruit that lasts long into the future—into eternity, in fact.

## 4

# Helping Each Other Run Well, Stay on Track, and Get Back on Our Feet

As we saw yesterday, there are different kinds of discipline. There's the discipline of training and practice, by which you learn to do something the right way. This is the kind of discipline professional musicians exercise when they spend hours every day practicing scales and arpeggios.

Another kind of discipline is correcting something that's wrong. A math teacher does this when she grades students' quizzes. All those red marks show the student what needs more work. A variation of this is pointing out errors ahead of time so that people avoid them, like you might point out potholes to avoid before someone drives down a back road.

God calls us to exercise all of these kinds of discipline in the church. We're to help each other learn to live rightly as Christians, warn each other not to fall into sin, and call each other back when we stray from the path.

### Helping Each Other Run Well ...

Read Ephesians 4:11-13. What are "the saints" (referring to all believers) called to do in their local churches? What's the goal of this?

Read Ephesians 4:15-16. How does the whole body grow to maturity in Christ? What part does each individual play?

What are some ways that you regularly speak the truth in love into others' lives?

How have others spoken truth in love into your life? What impact has it had on you?

Ephesians 4 calls us to build each other up in Christ by speaking the truth in love. All of us are to help our fellow church members grow in conformity to the character of Christ.

If the Christian life is a race, then we should all be both runners and trainers, running the race ourselves and helping others to run well.

### ... Stay on Track ...

Read Hebrews 3:12-13. What must we make sure isn't in us (v. 12)? What will an evil, unbelieving heart lead us to do (v. 12)?

What must we do in order to keep each other from departing from the living God (v. 13)? How often are we to do this (v. 13)?

Do you have people who regularly speak into your life about serious spiritual matters? People who would warn you if they saw your heart being hardened by sin?

If so, what are some ways those friends have helped to turn you away from sin? If not, pray that God would bring such people into your life. And write down below one way you plan to seek them out.

According to Hebrews 3, we must exhort each other to help prevent sin from entering our lives. If you see your fellow runner about to make a wrong turn and head the wrong way, stop him!

We might call this kind of discipline "preventive discipline." It's like giving each other a spiritual flu shot so that we don't let sin make us sick. In the church we must not only build each other up, but also help each other stay on track and not be led astray by sin.

## ... and Get Back on Our Feet

Read Galatians 6:1-5. What should those of us who are spiritual (that is, spiritually mature) do when someone is caught in sin (v. 1)? What does Paul tell us to do to ourselves as we're helping our brother or sister out of sin (v. 1)? Why?

What are we supposed to do with each other's burdens (v. 2)? What does that mean? Give practical examples.

Being restored from sin involves repentance, making amends for any harm it has caused, and being helped to live in new, fuller obedience to Christ. What are the difficulties involved in each of these steps? Why is it important that we help our fellow church members through these matters?

As we've seen in these passages, we all need help running the race of the Christian life.

- We need help to learn how to run well in the first place, so we are all called to build each other up through speaking the truth in love (Eph. 4:11-16).
- We need help staying on track and not being led astray by sin, so we are called to exhort each other daily (Heb. 3:12-13).
- And, when we fall into sin and are in serious danger of dropping out of the race altogether, we need brothers and sisters to come and help us get back on our feet, correct what went wrong, and to run along with us (Gal. 6:1-5).

In all of these different ways we are called to discipline one another in the church, so that every single member of the church would run well, finish well, and receive the prize God has in store for us (2 Tim. 4:6-8; Heb. 12:1-2).

# 5

# Dealing with Sin in the Church

The church is Jesus' embassy. He has authorized it to declare to the world who does and doesn't belong to him. So when someone joins the church, the church is saying, "Look, world! This is what a Christian looks like!"

At the same time, we know that not everyone who claims to follow Christ is a true believer (Matt. 7:22-25). Jesus made it very clear that those who don't obey His teaching aren't His disciples.

What then should a church do when someone claims to be a Christian and joins the church, but then quits living like a disciple of Jesus?

## Jesus' Instructions for Dealing with Sin in the Church

Read Matthew 18:15-17. What should you do if someone sins against you (v. 15)? What happens to this process if the person listens and repents (v. 15)?

What should you do if the person doesn't listen (v. 16)? What if he doesn't listen to the two or three others (v. 17)?

What happens if he doesn't listen to the church (v. 17)?

In this passage, Jesus teaches us what to do about sin in the church. He's specifically speaking about sin against ourselves, though it seems that this passage also has a broader application to any serious sins which may arise in the church. The goal of this whole process is to bring the offending individual to repentance. After all, we all sin, and we all need to repent. If someone sins

against you and then repents of it, you should forgive them and embrace them in love (Eph. 4:25). Case closed.

However, if the person doesn't repent, things get more serious. After all, Christians still sin, but we are characterized by repentance of sin and growing in obedience to Jesus' commands. If someone continues to hold on to their sin in the face of repeated rebukes from members of the church and ultimately the whole church, that calls into question their claim to follow Christ.

That doesn't mean that the church *knows* the person isn't a Christian, but it does mean that the church can no longer go on affirming this individual as a brother or sister in Christ. Hence, Jesus tells the church to treat such a person as an outsider, as someone who doesn't belong to the faith and therefore doesn't belong to the church.

Traditionally, Christians have referred to this as "excommunication." When a church member persists in unrepentant sin, the church should exclude them from their fellowship, which is seen most clearly in excluding them from the Lord's Supper, "ex-communion-ing" them.

Excommunication doesn't mean a person can't come to church. In fact, in most cases the church should want an excommunicated individual to come and sit under the preached Word so that it might lead them to repentance.

But it does mean that church members should no longer treat that person as a brother or sister. They should no longer have the kind of fellowship with them that they have with other Christians. They shouldn't act in any way that would indicate approval of their behavior, or that they still regard the person as a fellow Christian. Rather, apart from the case of a family relationship, interactions should be limited mainly to continuing to call the individual to repent and believe the gospel.

### Other Teaching on Discipline

We see this type of church discipline commanded in many other places in the New Testament.

- In 1 Corinthians 5, in language that strikingly parallels Jesus' teaching in Matthew 18, Paul commands the Corinthians to exclude from their fellowship a man who is sleeping with his father's wife.
- In Titus 3:10-11 Paul commands us to warn a divisive person multiple times and then after that having nothing to do with him.
- In 2 John 10-11 the apostle John warns us not to have any kind of fellowship with those who preach false gospels.

Why do you think so many churches fail to practice church discipline?

What do you think are the effects of failing to exclude those who sin unrepentantly from the church? (For Paul's perspective on this, see 1 Corinthians 5:6-7.)

What do you think are some of the benefits of practicing church discipline? (For one of them, consider what Paul says about elders who persist in sin in 1 Timothy 5:20.)

The goal of discipline is not punishment, but repentance and restoration (2 Cor. 2:5-8). When someone stops repenting of sin—which is to say, stops living like a Christian—the church needs to warn that person they are no longer living like a Christian, and it needs to treat the person accordingly.

While it seems mean and judgmental to some people today, this kind of church discipline is the most loving thing the church can possibly do to a person in that situation. After all, it is far better to be excluded from the church and thereby brought to repentance (like the man in 2 Corinthians 2) than to continue in sin and hear from Jesus on the last day,

***"I never knew you; depart from me" (Matt. 7:25).***

Just as God disciplines us in love and for our good, so the church is called to discipline its members. All church discipline—from preaching and teaching, to personal counsel, to public exclusion—is for the good of the individual and the good of the church.

Pray that God would use biblical, wise, and compassionate discipline to build up your church for His glory.

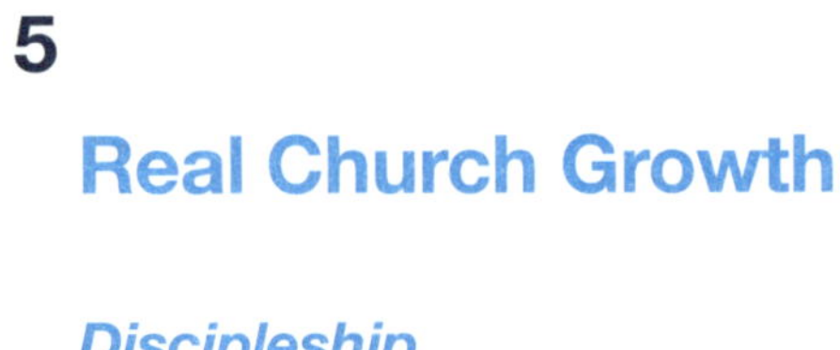

# 5

## Real Church Growth:

### *Discipleship*

# Getting Started

**Welcome back to your small-group discussion of *Church Essentials.* Begin your group by reflecting on the previous week's study.**

1 What are some things from this week's study that you'd like to discuss further or raise questions about?

2 What one truth sticks out to you from the study this week? What practical changes do you think God is calling you to make based on this study?

3 After this week's study, would you say that every Christian should be a member of a church? Why or why not?

4 How has your understanding of, and attitude toward, church membership changed because of this week's study?

5 What are some different aspects of discipline in the church? How can you personally participate in those in a regular, ongoing way?

6 In Matthew 18:17, Jesus commands the church to exclude a member who does not repent of sin. Based on your study, what does this mean? What is the purpose in such an act?

## View DVD Segment

**Watch the segment from the DVD using the viewer guide below.**

Making disciples is helping people follow JESUS.

Discipleship fundamentally happens through being CONVERTED.

Knowledge itself is no testimony to REGENERATION

All the images of the church in the New Testament are CORPORATE

The programs of a church try and create a framework on which a CULTURE can grow.

God WEIGHS our work rather than counts it.

People who make disciples are willing to radically REARRANGE their lives … and ask others to do the same.

Make sure you're not just reaching out to people who are just like YOU.

Someone who pushes for something they want is either not a Christian or really IMMATURE.

DISCIPLESHIP never goes only one way.

**Video sessions are available for purchase at lifeway.com/9marks**

## Group Response

**Discuss the segment with your group using the questions below.**

1 What does it mean to be a disciple of someone?

2 What are some ways we grow as disciples of Jesus? Are you taking advantage of those? Why or why not?

3 According to Mark Dever, what role should the church play in discipleship?

4 What kind of attitude and heart posture does it take to be a good disciple? Do those things come naturally to you? Why or why not?

5 Are you actively involved in discipling other Christians? What does that look like in your life?

6 What are some of the challenges of discipleship, both being a disciple of Jesus and helping others to follow Jesus?

**Close with prayer.**

# Session Five

## Real Church Growth

Healthy churches have a pervasive concern for church growth as growth is prescribed in the Bible. That means growing members, not just numbers.

Some today think that a person can be a "baby Christian" for a whole lifetime. Growth is treated as an optional extra for zealous disciples. But growth is a sign of life. If a tree is alive, it grows. If an animal is alive, it grows. If a person is alive spiritually, he or she grows.

That growth is called discipleship, and a healthy church creates a culture that is built around the spiritual growth of its members.

# 1

# What Does it Mean to Be a Disciple? Listen, Watch, and Follow

When Jesus wanted to train twelve men to carry out His mission, He called them to be His disciples (Luke 6:13). Following in their wake, the earliest Christians were known as disciples of Jesus (Acts 9:10, 26, 36).

In the ancient world, everyone knew what a disciple was, but in our society the idea isn't as common.

What do you think a disciple is?

Can you give some examples of *discipleship* from outside the church?

## Listen to Jesus' Teaching

Read Luke 6:40. What does Jesus call the person whom a disciple follows? What does this teach us about what it means to be a disciple?

The word *disciple* simply means *a student, a learner.* The first part of what it means to be a disciple of Jesus is simply to listen to Jesus' teaching.

Read Mark 1:14-15. How did Jesus begin His public teaching ministry?

What does this teach us about the first step in the Christian life?

Jesus began his ministry by urging people to repent and believe in the gospel. This means that, in order to become Jesus' disciples, we must repent of our sin and trust in Him. The way we become disciples of Jesus is by trusting in Him for salvation. This is what separates the disciples of Jesus from the disciples of anyone else. Jesus is far more than simply a teacher—He's our Savior and Lord.

What does it mean, practically, to listen to Jesus' teaching? Where do you find Jesus' teaching?

Is Jesus' teaching only found in the Gospels? (Hint: Read John 16:12-15. What does this teach us about the rest of the New Testament writings?)

Also consider John 5:39. Is there any part of Scripture that doesn't teach us about Jesus?

### Watch Jesus' Life

In the ancient world, disciples would learn not just from their leaders' teaching, but from their practical example. In this way discipleship is like apprenticeship. You learn how to be a woodworker not just by listening to what one says, but by watching him work every day.

So too, being a disciple of Jesus means watching Jesus' life.

Read Matthew 9:35-38. What does Jesus do in this passage?

Read Matthew 10:5-9. What does Jesus tell His disciples to do? How does this relate to what Jesus was just doing?

The disciples were with Jesus constantly. They heard Him teach. They saw Him heal. They saw Him have compassion on the crowds, who were like sheep without a shepherd (Matt. 9:36). Then Jesus told them to pray for God to send out workers into His harvest, and then He sent the disciples out to do as He did.

Obviously, we don't share the power and authority of Jesus' twelve disciples (Matt. 10:1). Not many of us will raise the dead. But, just like Jesus' disciples, we are to learn from Him by watching what He does.

**Follow in Jesus' Footsteps**

The point of watching Jesus' life, of course, is that we would then follow in His footsteps.

Read Luke 9:23-25. What does Jesus call us to do in this passage?

Read 1 Peter 2:21-25. According to Peter, why did Christ leave us an example (v. 21)?

What is the example Christ left for us (vv. 21-23)?

Christ's death paid the penalty for our sins so that we would be reconciled to God (1 Pet. 2:24-25). And it also leaves us an example of how to endure faithfully under persecution.

As Christians, we are to follow in Christ's footsteps not only in suffering, but in all of life. To be a disciple of Jesus means to follow Him, to walk in His footsteps, and to live as He lived.

We can do this because Jesus has given us the Holy Spirit to enable us to live a new life. And we are doubly motivated to do this because Jesus has died for us. Our obedience doesn't earn our salvation, it flows from it.

Is there anything about being a disciple of Jesus that is new or surprising to you? Why?

What aspects of being a disciple of Jesus are especially challenging to you? What are they? Why are they difficult?

What are some of the most exciting things about being Jesus' disciple? How do these motivate you to keep following Jesus in the long haul?

Being a disciple of Jesus means trusting Him for salvation, listening to His teaching, watching His life, and following in His footsteps. What a glorious calling God has given us in Christ!

## 2

# How to Grow as a Disciple: Instruction

A disciple is a learner, a student. To be a disciple is to be always growing in knowledge—knowledge that should be constantly transforming our lives.

Why do you think learning is such an important part of discipleship?

What happens to Christians who aren't continually learning God's Word better?

### Why Learning is Crucial to Discipleship

Read Acts 20:32. What is the Word of God's grace able to do to us?

Read John 17:17. How are we as Christians sanctified, or made more holy?

What do these two passages teach us about how we grow as Christians?

Learning is crucial to discipleship because God's Word is what builds us up and sanctifies us.

Read Romans 12:1-2? How are we transformed as Christians? What are we in danger of if we don't seek transformation by the renewing of our minds?

How do you regularly seek to renew your mind by God's Word?

Learning is crucial to discipleship because our minds lead the way for our lives. Transformed thinking leads to transformed living.

How does your thinking about who God is affect how you live? Give specific examples.

How does your understanding of the Bible's teaching about human nature affect how you live? Give specific examples.

How would your life change if you didn't believe that the Bible is true?

Learning is such an important aspect of discipleship because God is a God who speaks. He speaks for our conviction and comfort, our correction and encouragement. So we should diligently apply ourselves to the study of His Word as one of the main means He has given us for growing as disciples.

### Who Does the Teaching?

If learning is such an important aspect of discipleship, who does the teaching?

Read 1 Timothy 5:17 and Titus 1:7-9. Who in the church is called to labor in preaching and teaching?

How do you work to benefit from the preaching and teaching you hear every week? How do you seek to put it into practice?

God intends for godly, qualified elders to preach the Word week in and week out in the church. And he commands us to listen to them, honor them, and support them for their work. But pastors aren't the only ones who are called to teach in church.

Read Romans 15:14. Who does Paul expect to teach in the church?

Can you think of other members of your church besides your pastors who are filled with knowledge and able to instruct others? How do they teach others? How have you learned from them personally?

Why does it help to learn from a range of people in the church, including pastors and others?

One of the key roles of a disciple is learning from his teacher. Our Teacher, Christ, has given us many teachers in the church.

We should thank God for faithful elders who preach the Word to us regularly. And we should diligently pay attention to anyone in our churches who is filled with knowledge and able to teach others. As Paul says, do not be conformed to this world, but be transformed by the renewing of your mind (Rom. 12:2).

# 3

# How to Grow as a Disciple: Imitation

Have you ever heard the saying that some things are better caught than taught?

That's a helpful point, and no doubt it's true of many things. Especially with more practical skills, books and lectures can only take you so far. What will often be far more helpful is to attach yourself to someone who's skilled and experienced in whatever it is you're trying to learn, to observe them, and then to copy what they do.

What are some things that, in your own personal experience, have been better caught than taught?

Why do you think that it is important to learn these things by imitation, not just instruction?

As disciples of Jesus, we grow not only by instruction but by imitation. But His is not the only example we're called to follow.

### Timothy's Models

Read 2 Timothy 3:10-17. What had Timothy followed? List everything below.

What reasons did Paul give Timothy for why he should continue in what he had believed (vv 14-15)? (For background, see 2 Timothy 1:5.)

What impact did Paul expect the examples in Timothy's life to have on Timothy?

Timothy was facing opposition within the church and the threat of persecution from outside the church. So Paul reminded Timothy that he himself had been faithful through similar trials. And he reminded Timothy of the examples of the faithful lives of his mother and grandmother who taught Timothy the Scriptures from his youth.

These examples were meant to encourage and instruct Timothy. They were meant to remind him of how he should faithfully follow Christ. And they were meant to encourage him with the thought that, just as Paul and these two women had faithfully followed Christ, so also Timothy could remain faithful under pressure.

## The Benefits of Multiple Models

Read Philippians 3:17-4:1. Who did Paul call the Philippians to imitate?

Who else might influence the Philippians' actions (vv. 18-19)? What effect would this influence have?

Paul exhorted the Philippians not just to follow him, but also to follow all those who live according to the pattern that Paul set. What are some of the benefits of having multiple models in the faith?

Just like in 2 Timothy 3, in this passage Paul puts himself forward as a model for other Christians to follow, and he also directs their attention to others who faithfully follow Christ. As Christians, we are called to model our lives on those who model *their* lives on Christ. As disciples of Jesus, we should also be disciples of other disciples of Jesus. Christ is our ultimate example, but God has also given us godly examples within the church, and we should not neglect them!

Why is it important for you to have people within your church that you pattern your life on? In what ways can they teach you that a Christian who lives across the country can't?

What are some challenges in the Christian life that can be especially important to have living, in-person mentors help you walk through?

Who are some Christians in your church whose example you seek to follow? In what specific ways are they a model to you?

Think of members of your church who live exemplary, godly lives, but whom you only know from a distance. What are some ways you could get to know them better so that you could learn from them how to follow Christ more faithfully?

As Christians we grow by both instruction and imitation. The Christian life is both taught and caught. God has given us faithful models who walk in Jesus' footsteps, so that, by walking in theirs, we might learn better how to walk in the footsteps of Christ.

## 4

# A Culture of Discipleship

A culture defines what we think of as normal. It sets our habits and expectations. All of us live in a culture—or a number of overlapping cultures. Just as our society has a certain culture, our churches have their own cultures too. And we must be careful to shape our churches' cultures by God's Word.

Though church cultures might be diverse based on the configuration of each congregation, every local church should be characterized by a culture of discipleship.

In other words, it should be normal for church members to grow as Christians and help other members grow as Christians. It should be normal for you as a church member to seek out the teaching, counsel, and example of others, and to teach and model the faith to less mature believers as well.

### Older Teaching Younger

Read Titus 2:1-10. What different groups in the church did Paul address? What instructions did he give to each group?

What was Titus to show himself to be (v. 7)? Why is it important that church leaders serve as models to the congregation?

In this passage Paul gave specific instructions about how different groups of church members are to live out their discipleship to Christ within the church. And to one specific group, the older women, he gave the charge to teach the younger women in the roles that are uniquely theirs as wives and mothers.

All of us need help growing in Christ. Much of what that means is common to all Christians, but some of it is unique to different roles and responsibilities we fulfill.

Why do you think it is important for Christians to personally help each other grow?

Why is it important for women to disciple each other?

Why is it important for men to disciple each other? What are specific instructions you would give to older men discipling younger men?

What are some ways that people in your church are different from you? Why might it be helpful to be disicpled by someone who is different from you in significant ways?

**The Centrality of the Church in Discipleship**

Discipleship might happen through a number of different ways. It might occur through a Bible study ministry or a campus group. It might occur with a friend who goes to another church. It might happen as you, alone, read and process a book about the Christian faith.

While these kinds of discipleship efforts can bear good fruit, we shouldn't make any of them the *main* way we seek to grow in Christ. As we've seen in previous studies, that role belongs to the local church. And the church should be a good place for Christians to grow because discipleship is wired into its culture.

Read Ephesians 4:11-16. What is it that makes the body grow (v. 16)? Why, according to this passage, is it important that we are discipled in the church?

What is someone missing who pursues discipleship outside the church?

According to Ephesians 4:11-16, the church should be a place where Christians are constantly helping each other to grow to maturity in Christ. The body grows as each member contributes. And each member grows to maturity as the whole body grows. If discipleship is pursued outside the church you aren't just depriving yourself of the joy of being part of a growing body. You are cutting off one of the limbs that body needs to function.

What are some ways that a culture of discipleship should show itself in a church? How could you tell if it was there or not?

What's the difference between cultivating a culture of discipleship and having discipleship programs?

How do you contribute to your church's culture of discipleship? What more could you do?

In the church, discipleship relationships should be as normal as breathing. Discipleship in the church shouldn't merely be a program or an optional track, but instead a culture that permeates everything.

# 5

# Are You Making Disciples?

All living things grow. They may not grow all the time or grow at the same rate throughout their lifespan, but everything that's alive grows. This is as true of humans as it is of redwoods or golden retrievers.

It's also true of Christians. To be a Christian is to grow. Growth in grace is the sign of our life in Christ. Peter said that the qualities of faith, virtue, knowledge, self-control and much more should be ours and be increasing (2 Pet. 1:5-8).

But that's not all we can say about what it means to be a Christian. As we've seen throughout this study, to be a Christian is not merely to grow, but to help others grow.

Every disciple of Christ is called to make other disciples of Christ. Everyone who follows Jesus is called to help others follow Jesus. The New Testament includes no disciples who don't make other disciples.

## Others-Focused Growth and a Focus on Growing Others

Have you ever noticed how others-focused the New Testament's vision of the Christian life is?

Read Mark 10:42-45. How does Jesus define greatness?

Read Galatians 5:22-23. How many of these fruits of the Spirit can someone embody by themselves?

What are some things that make it difficult for you to manifest the fruit of the Spirit? What do those reveal about your own heart?

The New Testament's picture of Christian maturity is not a monk alone in the desert, but someone who is busy serving others. One of the key marks of a mature disciple of Christ is that they consistently sacrifice themselves for the good of others. And the New Testament gets even more specific about the good that we should aim at.

Read Romans 15:1-2. Who, according to Paul, should we strive to please (v. 2)?

For what purpose are we to please our neighbor?

To "build him up" means to help someone grow in maturity in the faith. (For more on this, see 1 Corinthians 14:12, 26.) What are some practical examples of ways that you can build others up in the faith? What can you do that will help someone else grow as a Christian?

As Christians, all of us should seek to serve others, especially our brothers and sisters in Christ (Gal. 6:10). This takes countless forms, including helping to provide for physical, material needs. But according to Paul in Romans 15, we should not simply seek to do good in general to our brothers and sisters in Christ, but also build them up in the faith.

Paul, then, expected every Christian to contribute to others' growth. For Paul, as for Jesus, Christians are disciple-making disciples. To be a disciple is to make disciples. Our growth in Christ is focused on others, and not simply on doing them good, but on helping them grow to maturity in the faith.

**Discipleship Made Simple**

Sometimes we make discipleship sound too complicated and intimidating. It can seem like unless you're a super-Christian, you have nothing to offer to your brothers and sisters in Christ.

But that's simply not true. If you're a Christian, then the Holy Spirit of God lives in you. And God the Holy Spirit surely has work to do, and things to say, through you, to the other members of your church. And the Holy Spirit has given us all spiritual gifts that we are to use for the common good, to build each other up (1 Cor. 12:7).

Discipleship can be as simple as going on a walk with someone and asking how you can pray for them. It can be a mother inviting a young single woman into her home and asking her questions about life while they do laundry together. It can be friends meeting up during their lunch break, reading Scripture together, and praying for the salvation of their coworkers.

Discipleship can take a thousand forms. The only necessary ingredient is that you're seeking to build up others in the faith.

Sometimes when we think about making disciples we only think about initial evangelism. Why is it important for all Christians to not merely share the gospel with others, but to continually help others grow in their likeness to Christ?

What are some ways you've grown as a Christian through trying to help others grow? Would you have grown in these ways if you weren't actively seeking to disciple others?

Think of one person in your church who is seeking to grow as a Christian, and whom you might be able to help along. Write down their name. Pray for them. Plan a time when you will reach out to them and encourage them in their faith.

According to the New Testament, a Christian is a disciple-making disciple. So pray that God would enable you to help others grow in Christ.

6

# Leading and Following:

## *Leadership in the Church*

## Getting Started

**Welcome back to your small-group discussion of *Church Essentials.* Begin your group by reflecting on the previous week's study.**

1 What are some things from this week's study that you'd like to discuss further or raise questions about?

2 What one truth sticks out to you from the study this week? What practical changes do you think God is calling you to make based on this study?

3 What are some new ways this week's study has challenged you to grow as a Christian?

4 Why, according to this week's study, should the church be the central context for your discipleship? What difference does that make?

5 Why is imitation important for discipleship? Who should we imitate? Should other Christians be imitating you?

6 What are some ways that you are seeking to make disciples of Christ?

## View DVD Segment

**Watch the segment from the DVD using the viewer guide below.**

We were made to FLOURISH under God's authority.

The abuse of authority is LYING about God in a particularly destructive way.

In the New Testament, when "pastor" or "elder" is mentioned it's always PLURAL.

The biblical qualifications for pastors or elders are the same qualities that should be found in every believer with two exceptions:

1. Not a recent CONVERT
2. The ability to TEACH

The naming of an elder is really only the RECOGNITION of what the congregation already knows to be true.

The New Testament difference between an elder and a deacon is the ability to TEACH.

The church member should submit to authority in such a way that it makes the work of an elder a JOY.

On earth, the congregation is the final JUDGE.

If the elders are the steering wheel, the congregation is the emergency BRAKE.

**Video sessions are available for purchase at lifeway.com/9marks**

# Group Response

**Discuss the segment with your group using the questions below.**

1 Do you think authority is good or bad? Why?

2 What, according to Scripture, are the responsibilities of pastors? Is this what you expect from your church's pastors?

3 Why is it important for a church to have multiple elders or pastors?

4 What kind of man should be an elder or pastor? How can you spot a man like this?

5 What's the difference between an elder and a deacon? What difference should that make in the church?

6 How does the character and gifting of leaders affect the church? What will happen if the men leading the church are not properly qualified?

# Session Six

## Leading and Following in the Church

What kind of leadership does a healthy church have? Is it a congregation that strives to ensure that the gospel is faithfully preached? Yes.

Is it deacons who model service in the affairs of the church? Yes.

But the Bible presents one more leadership gift to churches to help them become healthy: the position of elder or pastor, two words used interchangably in the New Testament.

This position is different from other positions of leadership. A healthy church recognizes the spiritual authority of its leaders and separates those leaders out for specialized service. In doing this, a church expresses its faith in God, who ultimately appoints these leaders, and its commitment to follow.

1

# Is Authority Good or Bad?

Many people today are skeptical of authority. They are wary of the corrupting influence of power. They are suspicious of the way that power can be used for self-serving ends at the expense of others. They resent being told what to do—even more, being made to do something by threat of punishment.

So a lot of people seem to want to do away with authority altogether.

Have your experiences with authority been primarily good or bad? How have they influenced your life and your view of authority?

While authority can certainly be abused, that's not the whole story. As Christians, we should embrace the proper exercise of authority, because God Himself has ultimate authority, and He has given certain kinds of authority to people.

## God Rules Over All

Read Daniel 4:34-35. What does Nebuchadnezzar confess about God in this passage?

What does Nebuchadnezzar say about God's relationship to people?

How does your heart react to the idea that God rules over everything and does all that He pleases in heaven and on earth?

God exercises absolute authority over the universe. He is the Lord of all, and His authority is perfectly good. He is never unjust. He never oppresses. He never abuses. He does whatever He pleases, and what he pleases is always right. In His authority, God has given authority to people for them to exercise. In fact, He's built that into our very nature.

Read Genesis 1:26-28. In whose image is man created (v. 26)? What does being made in the image of God mean for man's relationship to creation (vv. 26, 28)?

What do we learn about authority from this passage?

Have you ever considered before that exercising authority is part of our nature? How does that change your view of authority?

To be created in God's image means we represent God's rule on the earth. That means that authority, both having it ourselves and operating under it, is hard-wired into our humanity. Authority is built into our very nature. It's part of what it means to be human!

## God-Ordained Authorities: Government, Parents

God has given specific kinds of authority to different people and institutions.

Read Romans 13:1-7. Who, according to this passage, has God given authority to?

What does the government have authority to do (vv. 4, 6-7)? For what purpose (vv. 3-4)?

How does this passage call us to relate to the government (vv. 1, 6-7)?

God has given authority to human governments to punish evil and reward good. He's done this for a good purpose: that sin might be restrained and justice promoted. So we are called to submit to the government. Government authority can certainly be abused, but the authority itself is from God.

Read Ephesians 6:1-4. Who, according to this passage, has authority? Over whom?

What does a faithful exercise of this authority require (v. 4)?

How can parents' exercise of authority impact their children for the better? Has your own parents' authority been a blessing to you? How?

As we've seen, authority can be misused, but that doesn't make it a bad thing. Instead, authority is a good gift from God, who possesses all authority. It's given for the purpose of causing others to flourish, whether children, citizens, or any others who live under God-ordained authorities.

God's authority is good for us. And so are the authorities He has established.

# 2

# Elders: Called to Shepherd

In Scripture, God's people are often compared to sheep. We may think of sheep as friendly and cuddly, but that's because most of us haven't spent much time around them. Sheep aren't too bright, and they're very vulnerable. Sheep need to be led to food. They need to be protected from predators.

Ultimately, Scripture shows that God is the shepherd of His people (Ps. 23; Ezek. 34). He is the One who tends His flock like a shepherd, who gathers the lambs in His arms, and who carries them on His shoulders (Isa. 40:11). And Jesus tells us that He is the Good Shepherd who lays down His life for the sheep (John 10:14-18).

But in Scripture God also promises to send other shepherds to His people, men after His own heart, who will feed God's people with knowledge and understanding (Jer. 3:15).

So, in the New Testament, we see that one of the gifts Christ gives to His church is the gift of shepherds and teachers (Eph. 4:11). (Our English word *pastor*, in fact, comes from a word for *shepherd*.)

More often in Scripture, these men are called elders or overseers (Acts 14:23; Phil. 1:1; 1 Tim. 3:1-7; Titus 1:5-9; Jas. 5:14; 1 Pet. 5:1-4). All three of these terms (pastor, elder, overseer), refer to one role or office (Acts 20:17, 28). They all refer to those men who are charged to feed God's people with God's Word and to protect them from the enemies of their souls. While the whole church is ultimately responsible for its discipline and doctrine (Gal. 1; 1 Cor. 5), it is the elders who have a special responsibility to teach, shepherd, and exercise godly oversight over the church. They are the ones to whom God gives a special authority in the church.

## Elders: Called to Shepherd

Read Acts 20:17-38. Who did Paul call to meet with him in verse 17?

What did Paul charge these elders to do in verse 28? What motivation did he give for why they should be diligent to do this?

What threat to the church did Paul know would arise (vv. 29-30)? What did Paul urge them to do in response (v. 31)? How are they to combat this threat?

Why did Paul make such a big deal about his own example, both his teaching and his way of life (vv. 26-27,33-35)?

Write a job description for your pastors using only this passage. What things are at the top of the list?

Does this list differ at all from the things you expect your pastors to do?
If so, how?

Write our a prayer for your pastors. Pray they would be faithful to the task God has given them.

## The Pattern of Plural Pastoral Leadership

Once we understand that the most common term for "pastor" in the New Testament is actually "elder," we see more clearly that Scripture expects each church to have more than one. Look back through the references to "elders" and "overseers" given above. Notice how Scripture consistently speaks of a single church having multiple elders. It seems that the New Testament model of church involves shared pastoral leadership among a number of men.

Why do you think it's important for a church to have multiple elders?

What benefits do you think plural pastoral leadership brings to a church?

A plurality of leadership guards against potential abuses of authority. It also allows for a community of leaders to be in conversation with each other about the direction of the church. In such a group of men, there are a number of hearts tuned to hear the voice of God for the benefit of the church.

## Shepherds After God's Own Heart

Like shepherds of literal sheep, the pastors of our churches have a great responsibility. They have to faithfully feed us with the Word (Jer. 3:15; 1 Tim. 3:2). They have to resist and rebuke false teachers (Titus 1:9-10). They have to care for straying, sometimes ornery sheep (Acts 20:28). They have to watch over our souls as those who will give an account to God for how they have shepherded his people (Heb. 13:17). They have to set an example of godliness, integrity, and sacrificial service to the flock (1 Pet. 5:1-4).

Praise God for men who serve in this role faithfully. Pray for your pastors, that they would be shepherds after God's own heart.

## 3

# A Few Good Men: Qualifications for Elders

Being a pastor is not an easy task. It's certainly not for everyone. And if the wrong man steps into that role, it can do the church serious harm.

How do you think a church should determine who its pastors should be? What criteria should they use?

What do you think makes a good pastor?

Thankfully, God hasn't left it to us to decide what makes a good pastor—Scripture provides a clear set of qualifications for elders. They're found in both 1 Timothy 3 and Titus 1. Because the lists are almost identical, we're going to look at 1 Timothy 3 since it's a little fuller.

### Qualifications for Elders: Character

Read 1 Timothy 3:1-7. List each of the qualifications this passage gives for those men who would be elders.

"Above reproach" doesn't mean perfect, but it does mean that a man is free from any glaring sins in his life that call his overall integrity into question. What are some sins which you think disqualify someone from being above reproach?

What are some sins that you think don't disqualify a man from being above reproach? Give specific examples. (Remember, none of us are perfect!)

The Greek phrase translated "husband of one wife" could also be translated as "one-woman man" (v. 2). What does this qualification require of men who are married? What about of single men?

The words "respectable," "self-controlled," and "sensible" all refer to similar qualities (v. 2). List some examples of what they look like in daily life.

What do all of the qualifications listed in verse 3 have in common?

Why does Paul insist that a man must manage his household well in order to be an elder (vv. 4-5)?

Why would a recent convert be in danger of becoming puffed up with conceit and falling into the condemnation of the devil (v. 6)?

In verse 7, Paul insists that an elder must be well thought of by outsiders. Why do you think this is the case?

In verses 6 and 7, Paul twice warns against elders falling into Satan's traps. In what ways are elders especially susceptible to temptation?

Many people have observed that almost all of the qualifications for elders are required of all Christians elsewhere in the New Testament (Matt. 5:27-30; 1 Pet. 1:13; Titus 2:1-12; Rom. 12:13; Eph. 6:4; 1 Thess. 4:12). Apart from not being a new convert, the one thing that is not required of all Christians elsewhere is that elders must be "able to teach" (v. 2).

So, while elders are called to have *character* that should be exemplary for all Christians, they must have one specific *competence* that not every Christian will have.

### Qualifications for Elders: Competence

Read Titus 1:9-10. Why is it important that elders be able to teach, as 1 Timothy 3:2 says?

How can you tell if someone is able to teach the Word? What are practical ways of finding out?

Read 1 Timothy 3:4-5 again. Managing one's household well is obviously a test of character, but it is also a test of competence as well. What are some ways that a man's home life reflects his leadership abilities, or lack thereof?

Given that teaching ability and leadership in the home are qualifications for eldership, what does this say about how men who want to be pastors should prepare for ministry? How should the church help them in that?

**What are You Looking for in a Pastor?**

It's easy for churches to lose track of what to look for in a pastor. Sometimes we can get too focused on personality or past experience. Sometimes we look for a certain style of communicator or someone who's good at running programs.

What do you tend to look for in a pastor?

Do these biblical qualifications for elders challenge that at all? Do they change the emphasis, or draw your attention to things that you've overlooked?

God has told us in His Word what pastors need to do and be. Let's honor Him—and serve our churches—by praying that God would raise up such men, and keeping our eyes peeled for them.

## 4

# Deacons: Servants of the Church

Servants usually occupy some of the lower ranks of society. They do the work other people are too busy, or too refined, to do. They work out of sight, get paid little, have little freedom, and often have less dignity. Their work is often tedious, thankless, and practically endless.

Isn't it strange, then, that Jesus said He came not to be served, but to serve (Mark 10:45)? And in Mark 10:43-44, Jesus said,

***"Whoever wants to become great among you must be your servant, and whoever wants to be first among you must be slave of all."***

For Christians, service is greatness. The way down is the way up. If you humble yourself, God will exalt you. The path of following Jesus is the path of serving others, of putting their needs before our own.

What comes to mind when you think of servants, and service?

What comes to mind when you think of deacons in the church?

How does your answer to the first question compare with your answer to the second?

**Deacons: Servants of the Church**

The first thing to note about deacons is that the term *deacon* is simply borrowed from a Greek word that means *servant*. Beyond that, there are two key passages in the New Testament for understanding the role of deacons: Acts 6:1-7 and 1 Timothy 3:8-13.

## The Roots of Deacons: Trouble in the Church

Read Acts 6:1-7. What would "not be right" for the apostles to do (v. 2)? What did they intend to do instead (v. 4)?

What solution to the church's problem did the apostles propose (v. 3)? How did the church respond (vv. 5-6)? What was the result (v. 7)?

In this incident we don't necessarily see deacons appointed (these seven men weren't called deacons), but we probably see the historical origins of what later became the office of deacon.

The apostles, who were teaching and shepherding the church, needed to preserve both the unity of the church and their own ministry of prayer and preaching. So they appointed seven spiritually mature men to oversee this physical need of food distribution. As we'll see in a moment, this seems like the basic reason for deacons: to preserve the church's unity by handling its physical needs.

## Qualifications for Deacons

Apart from Philippians 1:1 (and possibly Romans 16:1) where deacons are simply mentioned, the only place in the New Testament where the word *deacon* is used as the title of a church office is in 1 Timothy 3:8-13.

Read 1 Timothy 3:8-13. What similarities do you see with qualifications for elders?

What do deacons who serve well gain for themselves?

There are two notable differences between the qualifications for elders and deacons that seem to hint at the distinction between their roles. First, while elders are required to be able to teach, deacons aren't. They're only required to hold firmly to the faith themselves (v. 9). Second, in 1 Timothy 3:5 Paul said,

***"If anyone does not know how to manage his own household, how will he take care of God's church?"***

Paul sees elders as having an overall shepherding role, giving oversight to the whole church like a father does to his household. Yet, while deacons do have to manage their households well (v. 12), Paul doesn't describe deacons as "caring for," that is, shepherding, the whole church. This seems to indicate that deacons, unlike elders, are *not* the overall spiritual leaders in a church.

When you combine these two differences, they make good sense. The way that elders lead the church is primarily through their preaching and teaching (1 Tim. 5:17). The office of deacon is not a teaching role, so it is also not a shepherding role.

## Defining the Role of Deacons

When we put all this together, we see that deacons are to be servants of the church. Like the men appointed in Acts 6, they should manage the physical needs of the church that demand attention. And they should do so in order to preserve the unity of the church and protect the elders' priorities of prayer and preaching.

What role do deacons play in your church? Does this line up with what we've seen in these passages?

What are some difficulties and challenges deacons face? How can you encourage them in their work?

Jesus is the greatest Servant. He gave His life so that we might live. He counted Himself as nothing so that we might receive everything in the life to come.

Praise God for servants in the church who mirror the service of Christ. And pray for your church's deacons, that they would serve your church as Christ has served us.

# 5

# How Well do You Follow?

Proverbs 14:28 says,

> ***"A large population is a king's splendor, but a shortage of people is a ruler's devastation."***

Leaders are nothing without followers. What good is a king without his subjects? What good is a teacher without a class? What good is a coach without a team?

All of us are called to serve each other in the church (Mark 10:43-44), and all of us are called to make disciples (Matt. 28:18-20). But not all of us are called to be a leader in the church.

What does that mean? It means that one of the most important tasks for most of us, leaders included, is that we *follow*, and follow well.

## Support

Read Galatians 6:6. What must the one who is taught share with the one who teaches?

What does it say about a church if their pastor lacks the money to properly support his family?

Read 1 Timothy 5:17-18. What are elders who rule well worthy of? What does that mean (v. 18)?

Do you consider it one of your responsibilities as a Christian to support your pastor financially? Why or why not?

Scripture is crystal clear: those who preach the gospel full-time deserve to make their living from the gospel (1 Cor. 9:14). So provide for your pastors. Give generously. And do what you can to make sure that your church is paying your pastors enough.

**Submit**

Read Hebrews 13:17. What does this passage call us to do?

What reasons does this passage give for why we should submit to our leaders?

What are some ways that you could make your pastors' job a burden? How would that negatively affect you, and other church members, in the end?

How can you make your pastors' job a joy, not a burden? What benefits will that bring to you and your church? Give specific examples. Pray that God would enable you to do this.

God calls us to submit to the elders of our churches. They watch over our souls as those who will give an account to God. So it will be to our advantage to make their job a joy.

### Respect and Esteem

Read 1 Thessalonians 5:12-13. What two commands did Paul give us about how we should relate to our leaders?

Why should we esteem our pastors highly (v. 13)?

What are some practical examples of respecting and esteeming church leaders? Do you do these?

To be a godly follower means that we support our leaders, submit to them, and respect and esteem them in love. Our shepherds keep watch over our souls as those who will give an account to God. They labor among us in the Word and doctrine. They teach, admonish, and care for us.

Praise the Lord for faithful shepherds. And pray that you and all the members of your church would make your pastors' job not a burden, but a joy.

NOTES

Building Healthy Churches

# HOW WILL YOU HELP YOUR CHURCH BECOME MORE HEALTHY?

9Marks exists to equip church leaders with a biblical vision and practical resources for displaying God's glory to the nations through healthy churches.

To that end, we want to see churches characterized by these nine marks of health:

1. Expositional Preaching
2. Biblical Theology
3. A Biblical Understanding of the Gospel
4. A Biblical Understanding of Conversion
5. A Biblical Understanding of Evangelism
6. Biblical Church Membership
7. Biblical Church Discipline
8. Biblical Discipleship
9. Biblical Church Leadership

Join us at **www.9marks.org**